RESEARCH HIGHLIGHTS IN SOCIAL WORK 25

Development in Short-Term Care
Breaks and Opportunities

Edited by Kirsten Stalker

Jessica Kingsley Publishers
London and Bristol, Pennsylvania

Research Highlights in Social Work 25
Editor: Kirsten Stalker
Secretary: Anne Forbes
Editorial Advisory Committee:

Professor J. Lishman	Robert Gordon University, Aberdeen
Ms M. Buist	University of Stirling
Ms A. Connor	Lothian Health, Edinburgh
Mr D. Cox	Robert Gordon University, Aberdeen
Mr K. Foster	Fife Region Social Work Department, representing Social Services Research Group – Scotland
Ms I. Freeman	Strathclyde Region Social Work Department
Mr M. King	Northern College, Aberdeen
Mr N. Munro	Robert Gordon University, Aberdeen
Dr F. Paterson	Social Work Services Group, Scottish Office
Dr A. Robertson	University of Edinburgh
Professor G. Rochford	Emeritus Professor, University of Aberdeen
Dr P. Seed	University of Dundee

Robert Gordon University
School of Applied Social Studies
Kepplestone Annexe, Queen's Road
Aberdeen AB9 2PG

First published in the United Kingdom in 1996 by
Jessica Kingsley Publishers Ltd
116 Pentonville Road
London N1 9JB, England
and
1900 Frost Road, Suite 101
Bristol, PA 19007, U S A

Library of Congress Cataloging in Publication Data
Stalker, Kirsten.
Developments in short-term care: breaks and opportunities/Kirsten Stalker
p. cm.-- (Research highlights in social work: 25)
Includes bibliographical references and index.
ISBN 1 85302 134 2 (pb: alk.paper)
1. Handicapped – Respite care – Great Britain. 2. Respite care – Great Britain.
3. Caregivers – Services for – Great Britain.
I. Title. II. Series
HV1559.G6S73 1995
362.4 0486 0941--dc20

British Library Cataloguing in Publication Data
A CIP catalogue record for this book is available from the British Library

ISBN 1 85302 134 2

Printed and Bound in Great Britain by
Cromwell Press, Melksham, Wiltshire

Contents

Introduction

Kirsten Stalker

Services providing short-term care are a relatively new phenomenon. Over the last 15 years or so, they have increased dramatically, with 'respite' now being seen as an essential component of community care. It is a matter of some concern, however, that this rapid expansion of provision and widespread acceptance of the concept have taken place in the absence of much systematic research. Although many agencies have carried out 'in-house' evaluations, the level of independent research is comparatively low. A key objective of this volume is to make the findings of the research which has been carried out more accessible to planners, policy-makers, practioners, students and, to a lesser extent, since the book is not specifically aimed at them, service users and carers.

This volume is the first publication in Britain to present an 'anthology' of research into short-term care. It covers a wide range of issues and various user groups. At the same time, a number of common themes run through the chapters. These are:

- an emphasis on the importance of short-term care providing a positive experience for the individual, as well as a break for carers;
- a focus on users' views;
- the need for cultural sensitivity within services, particularly given the evidence available that people from black and minority ethnic groups are not well served by current provision;
- a focus on progressive practice and innovative models of support.

Structure of the book

The opening chapter offers an overview of short-term care, intended to provide a context in which subsequent chapters can be located. It

1

traces the development of short-term care, discusses its objectives and outlines the various types of provision available. It goes on to discuss the social policy background, and the research evidence concerning the benefits, drawbacks and limitations of short-term care.

The next two chapters are exclusively concerned with users' views. Chapter 2 is written by members of the Holt Hall Self-Advocacy Group with Margaret Flynn, and powerfully presents, in written and pictorial form, their experiences and thoughts about short-term care services. Chapter 3, by Philippa Russell, herself a parent, presents a wealth of detailed information about the perspectives of parents using services, often in their own words.

Chapters 4 and 5 are concerned with two issues of key relevance to service development, irrespective of user group or providing sector. The former, by Anne Netten, deals with costings; the author outlines the theoretical background and basic principles of costs research, then describes how these were applied in a study of innovative ways of providing breaks. In Chapter 5, Meg Lindsay discusses 'the conundrum of quality', arguing that judgements are often based on false premises: it is essential to be clear about the specific purpose of any service, and the means chosen to achieve it, before identifying appropriate indicators by which to judge its performance.

Chapters 6 to 9 each deal with provision for a particular user group. Carol Robinson describes the range of services available to children with disabilities, discusses who uses them and why, before outlining some innovative initiatives in the UK, Scandanavia, Australia and the US. Marie Bradley and Jane Aldgate focus on short-term care for 'children in need', in this case meaning those facing social disadvantage. In Chapter 7, these authors present the findings of a four-year study examining support to 60 families. The research on short-term care for people with dementia is reviewed by Carole Archibald in Chapter 8. The findings in this area have to some extent proved conflicting and inconsistent: the author draws some useful conclusions across what has sometimes appeared to be a confused arena. Short-term care for people with mental health problems is poorly developed and often available only in hospital wards. In Chapter 9, Alison Petch presents the findings of a consumer survey conducted in Cairdheas House, a unique guest house in Edinburgh offering planned short breaks.

In the concluding chapter, Margaret Flynn, Lesley Cotterill, Lesley Hayes and Tricia Sloper discuss the results of a study examining innovative services to adults with learning disabilities. These schemes, characterised by a 'person-centred' approach, all have a focus on leisure and recreational activities. The authors underline the importance of services offering opportunities compatible with the known prefences and aspirations of people with learning disabilities.

The alert reader will have noticed that there is no piece within this volume on breaks for disabled people (i.e. those with physical and/or sensory impairment). Although many disabled people do receive short-term care – nearly always in inappropriate settings – there are considerable objections within the disability movement to the concept – and practice – of short-term care, as outlined in Chapter 1. Two writers were invited to contribute a chapter setting out this view in more detail, both declined: one, on the grounds that it was inappropriate to include any sort of 'disability' piece in a book on this subject; the other, because of the lack of evaluations to date carried out by disabled people themselves. In the light of these responses, a decision was taken not to include a chapter on this topic.

Terminology

Another contentious issue in this field, as in many others, is that of terminology. The services which are the subject of this book are often referred to as 'respite'. This is a term, however, which can be seen as carrying negative connotations (see Chapter 1) and some service users have said they prefer the word 'breaks' (see Chapter 2). This continuing debate is reflected in the pages of the present volume. Most contributors have not used the word 'respite'; a few have, and have explained their reasons for doing so. While there may be agreement about what Meg Lindsay calls the 'pejorative nature' of the term, there is less consensus about an acceptable alternative. Changing names does not of course alter reality. Although this book includes a focus on innovative ways of providing breaks, many people still receive 'respite' care in hospital wards or long-stay institutions. It may be only when all short-term care services prioritise the objective of offering people enjoyable breaks and stimulating opportunities, that the terms used to describe them will seem less important.

Acknowledgements

Finally, as editor of this volume, I would like to thank Joyce Lishman, Editor of the series, and Anne Forbes, Secretary to the project, for their guidance, support and practical assistance. I am also grateful to Margaret Flynn for her helpful suggestions on some aspects of the book's content. Lastly, thanks to all the contributors for their thoughtful pieces.

Chapter 1

Principles, Policy and Practice in Short-Term Care

Kirsten Stalker

The White Paper 'Caring for People: Community Care in the Next Decade and Beyond' (1989), which preceded the National Health Service and Community Care Act (1990), sets out six key objectives for service delivery. The first of these is: 'to promote the development of domiciliary, day and respite services to enable people to live in their own homes wherever feasible and sensible', and the second, 'to ensure that service providers make practical support for carers a high priority' (1.11). Thus, short-term care is being promoted as a cornerstone of community care policies. Services providing short breaks are proliferating, government guidance on standards has been issued (Social Services Inspectorate 1993) and short-term care is likely to become an increasingly common component of individual care packages. Any activity which supports carers, while also offering a positive experience to service users, is to be welcomed; there may, however, be a danger of short-term care becoming a standard response to a wide variety of differing needs and circumstances. Campbell's warning (1983), that short-term care should not be uncritically accepted as 'a good thing', still has resonance today.

This chapter begins by outlining the emergence of short-term care, discusses its main objectives and describes the range of services available for different groups of people. Second, the current social policy background is discussed, along with the impact of recent legislation on developments in the field. Third, the potential benefits, drawbacks and limitations of short-term care are explored, along with key aspects of quality and good practice. It is hoped that this overview will provide a context in which subsequent chapters in this volume can be located.

The development of short-term care

A number of factors can be identified which underlie the emergence of short-term care. Disillusionment with institutional settings as a suitable environment in which to bring up children, highlighted by the work of King, Raynes and Tizard (1971), and Oswin (1971), led to many more disabled children being cared for at home by their families. Concerns also emerged about institutional care for adults, following a number of hospital scandals (for example DHSS 1969, Cmnd 3975) and the publication of research which laid bare the bleak and deprived existence often led by long-term residents (Morris 1969). The advent of normalisation (Wolfensberger 1972) and 'ordinary life' principles (Ward 1982) has radically altered the nature of service provision, initially for people with learning disabilities, but increasingly for other groups as well. As has been widely documented elsewhere (Finch and Groves 1983, Glendinning 1983, Qureshi and Walker 1989) the policy of community care places a central emphasis on the role of families in looking after their disabled or older members. A burgeoning literature on the needs of carers has highlighted the demands and strains of their role (Wilkin 1979, Briggs and Oliver 1985, Twigg 1992) and, to a lesser extent, the rewards (Beresford 1994). At the same time, research has shown that the contemporary family receives little practical assistance in caring from its neighbours and less from friends (Osborn, Butler and Morris 1984). When asked what type of service would be most useful, carers have repeatedly identified short-term care as a priority.

It would be wrong to imply, however, that short-term care is a totally new phenomenon. Oswin (1984) provides an excellent account of the development of the service for children with learning difficulties. A not dissimilar account in relation to older people is given by Nolan and Grant (1992). During the 1940s and early 1950s, both children and older people were entering hospital for 'relief' care, on an informal basis. A circular issued by the Ministry of Health in 1952 regularised such admissions in respect of so-called 'mental defectives', while a circular appearing in 1957 noted the value of 'a short stay in hospital or Part III accommodation' for older people and their carers (Ministry of Health 1957). The 1963 Children and Young Persons Act empowered local authorities to give 'assistance' to parents in order to prevent their children being received into care. The wording of the Act, however, suggested that such assistance would be in the form of material help and for several years to come it was the health service which continued to be the main provider of short-term care.

Within Europe, Scandinavia has consistently led the way in terms of innovative services; Sweden, for example, pioneered the use of 'ordinary flats' on residential estates for short-term care 25 years ago (Evans and Fyhr 1978). In Britain, a series of policy documents issued during the 1970s acknowledged carers' need for regular breaks and/or recommended development of 'respite' services (DHSS 1971, Committee of Enquiry into Child Health Services 1976, National Development Group 1977a, 1977b, Scottish Health Service Planning Council 1979, Committee of Enquiry into Mental Handicap Nursing and Care 1979). Short-term care gradually became available in a range of local authority settings. In 1983, Allen reported that respite stays accounted for 58 per cent of all admissions to local authority Part III homes.

Innovations in the field of child care, including the adoption of youngsters with severe disabilities and the development of short-term and specialist foster-care, paved the way for the emergence of family-based respite care, the first British schemes being established in Somerset and Leeds in 1976. These schemes link people, on a one-to-one basis, with a local family or individual specially recruited to provide short-term care, usually in their own home. At national level, this type of care mushroomed dramatically during the 1980s. Such growth is to be welcomed, since family-based schemes generally offer the most homely and 'individualised' form of care, but at the same time, their development has been *ad hoc* and unstructured. Indeed, until relatively recently, there was no clear research evidence of the strengths and limitations of short-term care, nor any coherent social policy framework. This has led to tremendous variation at local level in almost every aspect of the schemes' organisation, but particularly in relation to the fees paid to link families. For example, a national survey found that payments for providing a 12-hour session of care range from £4.50 to £18.00, the average rate being £10.65 (Beckford and Robinson 1993).

What is 'respite care'?

It is becoming increasingly difficult to offer a satisfactory definition of 'respite care', since that term is often loosely used to denote some or all of a constantly expanding variety of services, with a range of aims. Some would argue that the term be reserved for services which provide overnight care as opposed to daytime provision; others distinguish between 'away-from-home' and domiciliary services. Numerous studies have shown that flexibility and the capacity 'to fit into an ordinary life' are vital ingredients of a good service (Fenwick 1986, Swift, Grant and McGrath 1991), indicating that as broad a definition as possible is desirable. The Social Services Inspectorate (SSI), in its recently issued *Guidance on Standards in Short-term Breaks* (1993) offers the following useful definition:

> 'An arrangement whereby children and adults normally dependent on regular carers for at least some aspects of their personal care and support, are provided with a break from their primary carer for a short period. This may include residential, domiciliary and home-supported assistance... It will not exceed three months for adults and no more than four weeks continuous care for children.' (SSI 1993, p.4)

The SSI deliberately avoided using the term 'respite care', because this may carry negative connotations. Indeed, the meaning of 'respite' is 'temporary cessation of something that is tiring or painful, postponement requested or granted; temporary suspension of the execution of a criminal; suspension of labour' (Chambers 1985), clearly implying a less than positive view of the caring role. For this reason, some services are using terms such as 'Shared Care', 'Breaks and Opportunities' or 'Community Links'. However, the whole concept of short-term care remains unacceptable to people within the disability movement, who perceive it as resting on a view of the individual as a burden from whom the rest of the family must have continual breaks if it is to continue coping (Hampshire Centre for Independent Living 1990). In this analysis, 'respite care' is equated only with crisis management, representing a failure to provide the individual with secure and adequate support. Rather than spending money on a service which perpetuates individuals' dependency, financial assistance should be given to people to buy services of their own choice, thus promoting independence and user control. In relation to many disabled people, this argument cannot be disputed.

The perception of short-term care as primarily for carers' benefit strongly persists. This may be justified as a moral imperative (Packwood 1980, Moriarty, Levin and Gorbach 1993) or on pragmatic grounds, aimed at perpetuating the activities of carers and thus reducing demands on state provision. However, the relationship between short- and long-term care is complex and hard to measure. Some commentators (Oswin 1984, writing about children with learning disabilities and Levin, Sinclair and Gorbach 1989, writing about confused older people) have suggested that a series of short-term admissions may precipitate long-term admission, while others, such as Nolan and Grant (1992), evaluating a hospital service providing care for older people on a rota basis, found otherwise. Archibald, in her chapter in this volume reviewing the literature in respect of people with dementia, concludes that while short-term care may not prevent long-term admission, overall it has a delaying and rationing effect.

More recently, greater emphasis has been placed on the aim of providing an enjoyable and beneficial experience for the individual receiving short-term care, particularly in provision for disabled children and adults with learning disabilties. This aspect of the service is one which often does not receive sufficient attention. It is a cause for some concern that short-term care is sometimes presented in the literature solely as a service for carers, with little or no attention being placed on the user's response (see, for example, Twigg 1992, Thornton 1989). Indeed, it could be argued that ensuring a positive experience for the individual should be the first principle of good practice. A number of studies have shown that, if offered a choice, adults with learning difficulties do not favour buildings-based services, but prefer 'ordinary' holidays such as youth hostelling or daytime recreational activities, alongside others, but not in segregated groups (Welsh Office 1991a). The opportunity to make new friends and improve their social life is valued by some (Fenwick 1986), while others would prefer to stay at home, with carers coming in to relieve their parents (Welsh Office 1991a, SSI 1991).

Flynn and the Holt Hall Advocacy Group (1994) not only document the dissatisfaction and unhappiness felt by some people in conventional 'respite' services, but also record users' views of the principles and practice which should inform provision for short breaks (see also Chapter 2 of this volume).

Range of services available

Even today, hospitals still provide a substantial amount of short-term care, although the people entering them are not ill and such institutions are not designed to meet the social or recreational needs of healthy people. It is particularly difficult to measure the extent of such admissions, however, as pseudo-medical reasons may be recorded in hospital records (Oswin 1984, Robinson and Stalker 1989). However, Information and Statistics Division (ISD) figures for 'holiday admissions' in Scotland show that 10,259 such admissions took place in 1991, comprising older people, those with dementia, learning disabilities and mental health problems. In each group there was a significant increase in admissions since figures were previously recorded, in 1987 (quoted in Lindsay, Kohls and Collins 1993). Comparable figures are not collected by the Department of Health in England, indicating a substantial gap in available information about short-term care.

Unfortunately, some children in Britain still enter hospital for short-term care, although this practice is decreasing. These include children with multiple and profound disabilities, sometimes with complex medical conditions, some of whom are very young (Robinson and Stalker 1989). Often they are receiving short-term care in the hospitals where they were born because parents have confidence in the staff's ability to care for their children.

Short-term care is provided in a range of residential settings, run by health authorities, trusts, voluntary bodies and some privately owned organisations, but principally by local authorities. In most cases, however, these short-term places are located within long-term facilities. Comprehensive figures are not available across sectors and user groups, but Lindsay et al. (1993) identified 783 establishments in Scotland offering short-term care, of which only 4 per cent were respite-only, 37 per cent had some beds designated for that purpose and the rest offered short-term care only when a long-term bed became vacant. Such 'mixing' is an unsatisfactory arrangement, often causing disruption to long-stay residents while also failing to meet the needs of 'respite care' guests (Allen 1983, Leonard 1991).

Among the 783 homes identified by Lindsay et al., 80 per cent were for older people and 14 per cent for people with learning disabilities. Recent research in England (Hayes, Flynn, Cotterhill and Sloper 1995) has collected comparable data relating to adults with learning disabilities, but, again, there is a dearth of readily available information for all user groups at a national level.

A survey carried out by the National Association of Family-based Respite Care, now called Shared Care UK (Beckford and Robinson 1993) identified 331 such schemes for children and adults with learning difficulties throughout Britain. Approximately 10,000 children were using this service in 1992, representing less than 6 per cent of the 169,000 judged to be most severely disabled (Office of Population Censuses and Surveys (OPCS) 1989). Only 3000 adults were using family-based schemes. Ninety-one per cent of children's schemes had a waiting list, the average number of children waiting being 18 per scheme. Shared Care Scotland (1994) has recently identified 27 family link schemes in Scotland.

Although the majority of family-based schemes cater for children with learning difficulties, a sizeable proportion cater for other groups, particularly older people and adults with learning difficulties. The House of Commons Select Committee on Social Services (1984) recommended the service be extended to cater for children 'at risk' as a preventive measure, while the Children Act (1989) obliges local authorities to provide support services for children 'in need'. Thus, schemes are now available for families living in social isolation, in continuing poverty, to relieve sick parents or to offer adolescents a break from stressful family situations (Aldgate and Bradley 1992; see also Chapter 7 of this volume).

Attempts are also being made to develop alternative models of family support which focus primarily on providing an enjoyable and stimulating experience for the individual. These include a variety of domiciliary care schemes whereby carers will go to the family home to perform a range of domestic and/or personal care tasks or else accompany the individual on short outings. Befriending schemes, generally aimed at older teenagers and adults, link the service user to a volunteer on a one-to-one basis. They regularly spend a few hours together during the day (overnight stays are less common) with a focus on shared interests and use of mainstream community facilities. Daycare can be offered to under-fives in a variety of settings, for example, with a childminder, in a nursery or 'opportunity group' (integrated play-group). These options, however, are not widely available and are often aimed at non-disabled children. Holiday playschemes and activity holidays for school-aged children are becoming more popular, often funded by local authorities, but organised by a voluntary or private organisation (see, for example, Stalker 1992). The potential of main-stream recreational activities, such as youth clubs or sports centres, as a source of short-term care is gradually gaining more recognition (Marchant 1993), but, again, is not well developed across the country. Overall, the more innovative schemes tend to cater for children: there is an urgent need to create a wider range of attractive, age-appropriate opportunities for adults.

As the above account indicates, development of short-term care services to date has focused on the needs of older people (including those with dementia) and children and adults with learning difficulties. Services to disabled people and those with mental health difficulties are much less developed, perhaps partly because short-term care is seen as being less appropriate to their needs. Hospitals still provide the bulk of short-term care for people with mental health problems: 6 per cent of all admissions to Scottish psychiatric hospitals in 1990 (representing about 2000 people) fell into this category. (Again, these figures are not available for England.) Befriending schemes do exist, however, run mainly by voluntary organisations such as the Mental Health After Care Association. A guest house run by the Penumbra organisation in Edinburgh aims to provide an alternative to hospital, by offering planned breaks for users and carers (see Chapter 9 of this volume). It is, however, probably unique in Britain.

Lindsay *et al.* (1993) identified 30 facilities in Scotland offering short-term care to disabled adults, and a further four to children. A major concern must be that most of this provision is in hospitals and nursing homes and therefore quite inappropriate. Furthermore, only three adults' services, and one for children, were 'dedicated' to short-term care. Others either had a small number of beds set aside for this purpose, or else provided it as and when space was available. In a recent study of support to disabled people in Scotland (Stalker with Reddish 1995), the only examples of good practice identified in this field were two four-bedded 'ordinary' houses (in different locations), run by Grampian Living Options Ltd, an independent organisation which includes disabled people among its directors. These facilities offer an excellent model of support which could usefully be emulated elsewhere.

Social policy framework

Children's services

Until 1991, short-term care for children was generally provided in England and Wales under the National Health Service Act 1977, which enabled local authorities to provide support services free of charge, without formally receiving children into care. At its best, this model provided an example of genuine partnership between professionals and parents, who found its informal, non-bureaucratic nature very attractive (Robinson 1987, Swift, Grant and McGrath 1991). At the same time, the lack of a clear social policy framework noted earlier led to short-term care being largely unregulated, with services showing marked variation in their operation.

Until 1995, short-term care was provided in Scotland under the liberal provisions of the Social Work (Scotland) Act 1968. This has been replaced by the children (Scotland) Act 1995, which introduces a new duty for local authorities to provide services for 'children in need', including those 'with, and affected by, disability' (Section 23). The legislation makes no reference to short-term care. The Government promised in Parliament, however, that 'respite' services would be specified in children's services plans.

As is often the case, legislative change came first to England and Wales. The Children Act 1989 (implemented in 1991) represents a landmark in relation to disabled children, since it brings them into mainstream childcare legislation from which, historically, they have been excluded (Shearer 1980). Under the Act, local authorities must co-operate with other agencies to provide preventive services for 'children in need', including those with disabilities. Short-term care clearly falls into this category, although again, it is not specifically identified.

Under the Family Placement regulations accompanying the Act, (Department of Health 1991) short-term care (in this case meaning any child receiving at least 24 hours of care) became subject to the same regulations and checks as foster care. For example, every accommodated child must have a care plan, setting out the arrangements relating not only to short-term care, but also to his or her health and education. The regulations also required frequent reviews of each placement – three per year. Before embarking on short-term care, a child must have either a medical examination or a written report from a doctor. It was also specified that social workers must visit each child during their first overnight stay in short-term care. Furthermore, service providers were to issue extensive documentation in the form of written agreements, first, between agency and link family, second, between agency and parents or carer and third, relating to the individual child. If a young person was using more than one service for short-term care, which is by no means uncommon, the regulations were to be applied separately to each facility.

Research on services to disabled children (Robinson, Minkes and Weston 1993, Macadam 1993) suggested that the overall effect of these changes was to inhibit the informal, non-bureaucratic aspect of short-term care, which has been greatly valued by parents in the past, and to increase the workload of service providers to almost unmanageable proportions. Family-based schemes in particular tend to be under-resourced at the best of times. Macadam, in her survey of 216 such schemes, found that many of the new regulations were simply not being met by all the services. For example, only 21 per cent were issuing comprehensive care plans, while 48 per cent were using a plan relating only to short-term care arrangements. About a third of services had no plan at all. A further worrying effect of the new legislative framework was that over half the schemes in the survey reported no increase in the number of users since the Act was implemented, while 8 per cent had experienced a decline. This contrasts with a growth of 50 per cent in family-based care between 1989 and 1991 (Beckford and Robinson 1993). Robinson *et al.* (1993), evaluating the regulations' impact on residential short-term care, found that several key principles of the Children Act were not being implemented in practice, such as consulting children, minimising the effects of children's disabilities, promoting integration, partnership with parents and cultural sensitivity. The Department of Health later introduced amendments to these regulations, making them less burdensome to service providers (DOH 1995).

Services for adults

Despite the prominence given to short-term care within the White Paper, the National Health Service and Community Care Act 1990 was surprisingly silent on the subject. However, it introduced certain measures which may have significant effects on service delivery. To date, little systematic research has been carried out on the impact of the legislation on short-term care, although it is possible to speculate. Screening and assessment procedures, for example, have restricted direct access to short-term care, with individuals whose needs are deemed 'complex' receiving a holistic assessment. The increasing emphasis on targeting provision at those 'in greatest need' has led to services developing stricter criteria for eligibility. Thus, it is possible that the preventive, supportive function of short-term care may give way to a more crisis-oriented service. Evidence has emerged of a similar effect arising from the introduction of charges (Thomas 1994).

Under the National Assistance (Assessment of Resources) Regulations 1992, a local authority can charge a 'reasonable' rate for the first eight weeks of short-term care; after that, it must be subject to means-testing, in whatever sector it is provided. This has resulted in considerably increased charges for some users, but also, again, great disparity in the cost of short-term care in different parts of the country (House of Commons Health Committee 1993, Thomas 1994). In this sense, the legislation has, ironically, introduced a 'perverse incentive' in favour of hospital-based short-term care, which remains free of charge. 'Respite' beds are being reduced, however, and the extent to which funding for alternative provision within the community is included in resource transfer arrangements appears variable.

The final piece in the social policy jigsaw surrounding short-term care is the Registered Homes Amendment Act. Under this law, which came into effect in 1992, small homes (with up to four beds) and adult placement schemes, have to be registered with the local authority. Thus, regulations designed primarily for residential homes are applicable to private households. Authorities can, for example, charge carers an initial registration fee of up to £230. Again, it seems that this legislation may have the unintended effect of undermining the development of short-term care, while 'Caring for People' seeks to promote it.

Benefits and drawbacks of short-term care – implications for practice
A number of studies have shown that short-term care can have beneficial effects on carers, in terms of alleviating stress (Chetwynd 1985, Bose 1989) and allowing time for rest and relaxation (Joyce, Singer and Isralowitz 1983, Moriarty and Levin 1993). Additional reported benefits for carers include the freedom to pursue other activities, a sense of security in case of breakdown of usual care arrangements and improved family relationships (Welsh Office 1991b, Thornton 1989). Siblings of disabled children have also been shown to benefit (Oswin 1984), since their parents are able to spend more time with them and share certain activities which may prove difficult when the disabled child is present.

Various benefits have been identified for adults receiving short-term care. Allen (1983), investigating the experiences of older people entering residential homes, identified three groups who 'felt better' as a result – those who lived alone, those entering a 'holiday' home or similar facility and those whose relationship with their carers was tense. About a third felt better physically and a similar proportion, emotionally; that is, they felt more cheerful and confident. Others, however, were less happy. Likewise, Nolan and Grant (1992), evaluating a hospital rota bed scheme for older people, divided the users (N=30) into three groups, according to their perceptions of the service – about a quarter viewed it as a positive experience, a little over half 'tolerated' it as being for the benefit of their carers, while, for a fifth, short-term care was 'a totally negative' experience, since they felt abandoned by their carers. Some older people, particularly those suffering from dementia, appear to undergo a deterioration, rather than an improvement, in their abilities, some, for example, becoming incontinent or more confused (Eagles and Gilleard 1984, Moriarty *et al.* 1993).

Children using short-term care have been found to gain from the experience, through increased independence, improved skills and the opportunity for fun and enjoyment. In an evaluation of the Avon family-based scheme, some children were described by their social workers as being calmer and more relaxed after staying with their link family, while others were more alert and better stimulated (Robinson 1986). Other benefits reported by parents or scheme co-ordinators were more indirect, but of considerable significance – integrating children into mainstream society and helping to prevent family breakdown or child abuse.

However, some children suffer considerable distress and homesickness, not only in residential facilities (Oswin 1984), but also in family-based schemes (Stalker 1990). This is often related to the timing, length and frequency of visits, the nature of previous separations (homesickness being more likely where children have had experience of unhappy stays in hospital), the nature of the parent/child attachment, and inadequate preparation, including a lack of openness about arrangements. In one study of short-term care facilities in three English regions, over half the children (N=64) staying in local authority homes had no introductory visit prior to staying overnight for the first time (Robinson and Stalker 1990).

The planning and co-ordination of short-term care is sometimes poor, as Robinson documents in her chapter in this volume. In the study just quoted, four youngsters were found to have spent excessive lengths of time in 'short-term care', ranging from eight months to three years (the latter being a boy aged six in a hospital ward). It is this kind of irregularity which the Family Placement Regulations are intended to address, but, as already noted, not all service providers are managing to carry out regular monitoring and reviews. Furthermore, there is no equivalent legislative safeguard at present for children in Scotland, nor for adults generally.

Research suggests that the quality of care provided is generally of a high standard (Swift *et al.* 1991, Welsh Office 1991b, Robinson *et al.* 1993). There are exceptions, however. Hubert (1991), in a study of 20 families using short-term care in two health authority settings in the south of England, found a high level of dissatisfaction and anxiety among parents. Their sons and daughters were often left unoccupied for hours and it was not uncommon for young people in wheelchairs to be found soaked in urine or faeces.

There is ample evidence of inequality of access to short-term care. The people who tend to lose out are individuals with challenging behaviour, black and minority ethnic groups, low-income families, older children and adults, particularly men, and those with severe physical impairments (Orlik, Robinson and Russell 1991, Robinson and Stalker 1992a,b). These people are over-represented on waiting-lists for family-based respite care, more likely to use institutional provision, especially hospitals, rather than other facilities, and also figure highly among non-users of services. Baxter *et al.* (1990) identify three major issues which services must tackle in order to become more responsive to the needs of black families – information and communication difficulties, concerns about the appropriateness of care (for example, the opportunity for religious observance and dietary requirements) and the availability of black professionals and link families.

Finally, the Department of Health guidance on children with disabilities (1989), accompanying the Children Act, sets out the essential features of a good short-term care service. With some slight adaptation, it is equally applicable to adults' services. Short-term care should:

- be a local service
- provide high-quality care, with the individual seen as a person first and disabled second
- be available on demand
- meet the needs of *all* children (or adults)
- provide age-appropriate care
- be part of an integrated programme of family support.

Conclusion

This chapter has highlighted a number of issues arising from research which remain unresolved in practice. The dual nature of short-term care – its capacity to provide a positive experience for the individual, while also offering support to carers – requires greater attention. As part of this, further effort needs to be directed into developing a range of service options, including attractive, mainstream breaks and opportunities. The policy of providing short-term care within 'long-term' settings requires urgent review, the evidence being that dedicated short-term care units generally offer a more positive experience than those which strive to meet competing needs of long-stay residents and short-term guests. An appropriate balance requires to be achieved between the need for monitoring and safeguards on the one hand, while also allowing for flexibility and ease of access on the other. One way of achieving this would be to distinguish between regulations governing short- and longer-term care, with 'modified' regulations applying to the former. Finally, a number of issues discussed in this chapter – territorial injustice, insecurity of funding and the lack of comprehensive information at national level about scale of provision, number of users and amount of use – reflect the absence of a clear policy framework underpinning short-term care. It is difficult to avoid the conclusion that a stronger lead from central government is overdue.

References

Aldgate, J. and Bradley, M. (1992) 'The Respite Accommodation Study, Phase 1.' Report to the Department of Health, University of Oxford.

Allen, I. (1983) *Short-stay Residential Care for the Elderly*. London: Policy Studies Institute.

Baxter, C., Poonia, K., Ward, L. and Nadirshaw, Z. (1990) *Double Discrimination: Issues and Services for People with Learning Difficulties from Black and Minority Ethnic Communities*. London: King's Fund Centre.

Beckford, V. and Robinson, C. (1993) *Consolidation or Change?* University of Bristol: Norah Fry Research Centre.

Acknowledgements

Thanks to Carol Robinson and Roger Fuller for their helpful comments on this chapter.

Beresford, B. (1994) 'Resources and strategies: how parents cope with the care of a disabled child.' *Journal of Child Psychology and Psychiatry 35*, 1, 171–209.

Bose, R. (1989) 'Innovations in care for children with mental handicap.' *Mental Handicap,* 17 December, 167–170.

Briggs, A. and Oliver, J. (1985) *Caring: Experiences of Looking After Disabled Relatives.* London: Routledge and Kegan Paul.

Campbell, L. (1983) 'Too much of a good thing?' *Community Care 3,* 24–26.

Chambers Concise Twentieth Century Dictions (1985) Edinburgh: Chambers.

Chetwynd, J. (1985) 'Factors contributing to stress on mothers caring for an intellectually handicapped child.' *British Journal of Social Work 15,* 295–304.

Committee of Enquiry into Child Health Services (The Court Report) (1976) *Fit for the Future.* London: HMSO.

Committee of Enquiry into Mental Handicap Nursing and Care (The Jay Report) (1979) London: HMSO.

Department of Health (1989) *The Children Act 1989: Guidance and Regulations. Vol 6: Children with Disabilities.* London: HMSO.

Department of Health (1991) *The Children Act 1989. Vol 3: Guidance and Regulations to Family Placements.* London: HMSO.

Department of Health (1995) *The Children Act (Short-Term Placements).* (Miscellaneous Amendments Regulations). London: HMSO.

Department of Health and Social Security (1969) *Report of the Committee of Enquiry into Allegations of Ill-treatment of Patients and Other Irregularities at the Ely Hospital, Cardiff.* Cmnd 3975. London: HMSO.

Department of Health and Social Security (1971) *Better Services for the Mentally Handicapped.* London: HMSO.

Eagles, J. and Gilleard, C.J. (1984) 'The functions and effectiveness of a day hospital for the dementing elderly.' *Health Bulletins 2,* 87–91. Edinburgh.

Evans, R. and Fyhr, G. (1978) 'Sharing the caring: a Swedish approach to short term care of mentally handicapped children.' *Child: Care Health and Development 4,* 2, 69–78.

Fenwick, J. (1986) *Respite Family Care and Mental Handicap in Newcastle: An Evaluation of the FACE and STOP Schemes.* Newcastle Policy Services and Social Services Department.

Finch, J. and Groves, D. (eds) (1983) *A Labour of Love: Women, Work and Caring.* London: Routledge and Kegan Paul.

Flynn, M. and the Holt Hall Advocacy Group (1994) *Taking a Break: Liverpool's Respite Services for Adult Citizens with Learning Disabilities.* Manchester: National Development Team.

Glendinning, C. (1983) *Unshared Care.* London: Routledge and Kegan Paul.

Hampshire Centre for Independent Living (1990) 'Respite care', HCIL Papers.

Hayes, L., Flynn, M., Cotterill, L. and Sloper, T. (1995) *Respite Services for Adult Citizens with Learning Disabilities. Report to Joseph Rowntree Foundation.* Manchester: National Development Team.

House of Commons Health Committee (1993) *Community Care: The Way Forward,* Sixth Report. Vol 1. London: HMSO.

House of Commons Select Committee on Social Services (1984) *Children in Care, Second Report.* London: HMSO.

Hubert, J. (1991) *Home Bound: Crisis in the Care of Young People with Severe Learning Difficulties: A Story of Twenty Families.* London: King's Fund Centre.

Joyce, K., Singer, M. and Isralowitz, R. (1983) 'Impact of respite care on parents' perceptions of quality of life.' *Mental Retardation 21,* 153–156.

King, R.D., Raynes, N.V. and Tizard, J. (1971) *Patterns of Residential Care: Sociological Studies in Institutions for Handicapped Children.* London: Routledge and Kegan Paul.

Leonard, A. (1991) *Homes of Their Own: A Community Care Initiative for Children with Learning Difficulties.* Aldershot: Gower.

Levin, E., Sinclair, I. and Gorbach, P. (1989) *Families, Services and Confusion in Old Age.* Aldershot: Avebury.

Lindsay, M., Kohls, M. and Collins, J. (1993) *The Patchwork Quilt: A Study of Respite Care Services in Scotland.* Edinburgh: Social Work Services Inspectorate.

Macadam, M. (1993) 'The effects of the children act 1989 on short-term breaks for disabled children.' *Social Care Research Findings 32.* York: Joseph Rowntree Foundation.

Marchant, C. (1993) 'Time out.' *Community Care,* 2 December, 8.

Ministry of Health (1952) *Short-term Care of Mental Defectives in Case of Urgency.* Circular 5/52. London: HMSO.

Ministry of Health (1957) *Local Authority Services for the Chronically Sick and Infirm.* Circular 14/57. London: HMSO.

Moriarty, J. and Levin, E. (1993) 'Interventions to assist caregivers.' *Reviews in Clinical Gerontology 3,* 301–308.

Moriarty, J., Levin, E. and Gorbach, P. (1993) *Respite Services for Carers of Confused Elderly People*. London: National Institute of Social Work Research Unit.

Morris, P. (1969) *Put Away*. London: Routledge and Kegan Paul.

National Development Group (1977a) 'Mentally handicapped children: a plan for action.' NDGMH, Pamphlet No 2. London.

The National Development Group (1977b) 'Residential short-term care for mentally handicapped people: suggestions for action.' NDGMH, Pamphlet No 4. London.

Nolan, M. and Grant, G. (1992) *Regular Respite: An Evaluation of a Hospital Rota Bed Scheme for Elderly People*. London: Age Concern.

Office of Population Censuses and Surveys (1989) *Report 6. Disabled Children: Services, Transport and Education*. London: HMSO.

Orlik, C., Robinson, C. and Russell, D. (1991) 'A survey of family based respite care schemes in the United Kingdom.' University of Bristol: Norah Fry Research Centre.

Osborn, A.F., Butler, N.R. and Morris, A.C. (1984) *The Social Life of Britain's Five Year Olds: A Report of the Child Health and Education Study*. London: Routledge and Kegan Paul.

Oswin, M. (1971) *The Empty Hours*. Aylesbury: Pelican.

Oswin, M. (1984) *They Keep Going Away: A Critical Study of Short-stay Residential Facilities for Children who are Mentally Handicapped*. London: King's Fund Centre.

Packwood, T. (1980) 'Supporting the family: a study of the organisation and implications of hospital provision of holiday relief for families caring for dependants at home'. *Social Science and Medicine 14*, 613–620.

Qureshi, H. and Walker, A. (1989) *The Caring Relationship: Elderly People and Their Families*. London: Macmillan.

Robinson, C. (1986) *Avon Respite Care Scheme Evaluation Study: The Final Report*. Department of Mental Health, University of Bristol.

Robinson, C. (1987) 'Key issue for social workers placing children for family-based respite care.' *British Journal of Social Work 16*, 257–284.

Robinson, C. and Stalker, K. (1989) *Time for a Break: Respite Care – A Study of Providers, Consumers and Patterns of Use*. University of Bristol: Norah Fry Research Centre.

Robinson, C. and Stalker, K. (1990) *Respite Care: The Consumer's View*. University of Bristol: Norah Fry Research Centre.

Robinson, C. and Stalker, K. (1992a) *New Directions: Suggestions for Improving Take-up in Short-term Breaks*. London: HMSO.

Robinson, C. and Stalker, K. (1992b) *Why are We Waiting?: Reducing Waiting Lists – Practical Guidance for Developing Short-term Breaks*. London: HMSO.

Robinson, C., Minkes, J. and Weston, C. (1993) 'Room for improvement.' *Community Care 8*, July, 26–27.

Scottish Health Service Planning Council (1979) *A Better Life: A Report on Services for the Mentally Handicapped in Scotland (The Peters Report)*. Edinburgh: Scottish Office.

Scottish Office (1994) *Children (Scotland) Bill*. London: HMSO.

Secretaries of State for Health, Social Security, Wales and Scotland (1989) *Caring for People: Community Care in the Next Decade and Beyond*. London: HMSO.

Secretary of State for Scotland (1993) *Scotland's Children: Proposals for Child Care Policy and Law*. Edinburgh: HMSO.

Shared Care Scotland (1994) *Family Based: A Report on a Survey of Respite Care Schemes in Scotland*. Dunfermline: Shared Care Scotland.

Shearer, A. (1980) *Handicapped Children in Residential care – a Study of Policy Failure*. London: Bedford Square Press.

Social Services Inspectorate (1991) *A Report of a Seminar on Adult Placement Schemes: Their Future Contribution to Community Care*. Birmingham: Department of Health.

Social Services Inspectorate (1993) *Guidance on Standards in Short-term Breaks*. London: HMSO.

Stalker, K. (1990) *Share the Care: An Evaluation of a Family-based Respite Care Service*. London: Jessica Kingsley Publishers.

Stalker, K. (1992) 'Having a great time at Treworra.' *Mencap News*, 25 July, 8–9.

Stalker, K. with Reddish, S. (1995) *Supporting Disabled People in Scotland: An Overview of Social Work and Health Services*. Edinburgh, Scottish Office: HMSO.

Swift, P., Grant, G. and McGrath, M. (1991) 'Home to home: A review of family-based respite care in Dyfed.' Bangor: University College of North Wales.

Thomas, M. (1994) *Charging Older People for Care*. Edinburgh: Age Concern.

Thornton, P. (1989) *Creating a Break*. Mitcham: Age Concern England.

Twigg, J. (1992) *Carers: Research and Practice*. London: HMSO.

Ward, L. (1982) *People First: Developing Services in the Community for People with Mental Handicap*. London: King's Fund Centre.

Welsh Office, Social Services Inspectorate (1991a) *The Review of the All Wales Strategy: A View from the Users.* Cardiff: Welsh Office.

Welsh Office, Social Services Inspectorate (1991b) *The Review of the All Wales Strategy: A View from the Carers.* Cardiff: Welsh Office.

Wilkin, D. (1979) *Caring the Mentally Handicapped Child.* London: Croom Helm.

Wolfensberger, W. (1972) *Principles of Normalization in Human Services.* Toronto: National Institute on Mental Retardation.

Chapter 2

Taking a Break or Respite Services for Adults with Learning Disabilities

Angela Darnell, Ian Davies, Marilyn Pegram,
Peter Skilbeck and Jean Smith, Holt Hall Social Education
Centre, Liverpool, with Margaret Flynn, National Develop-
ment Team

Introduction

We are pleased to be asked to write this. We have done it because we have been doing a lot of thinking about respite services in Liverpool. We have visited places and some of us have gone into places. Our ideas matter. Margaret has written them down. They are in a book we wrote with her. Please read it. It's called *Taking a Break*. We prefer this name to 'respite' because it shows that we are having a break from what we do.

Respite places now

We do not think much of respite places. We have gone to some places where people have to share bedrooms with people they don't know. This is wrong. Some people have said it's like a holiday. It's not. We know some people like to get away from their families, but it could

Figure 2.1

be nicer. It's a shame that this is mostly the kind of thing people get. We're grown up and we should have our own rooms.

Things we need to talk about

Figure 2.2

Figure 2.3

We have been to places where people go to bed really early. Like in one place a man went to bed at 7 o'clock. No one said to him 'Here's some nice things to do.' People get really bored in respite places. When we went to one a woman wanted to leave with us and she was told she had to stay because there weren't enough staff.

Figure 2.4

Some people get hurt. It might be because someone gets upset and they hit. It means that sometimes we're not safe. Sometimes people get sent a long way away and that makes them really sad. They don't know anyone. We think it's wrong.

It's a shame that people who go to respite places have to go places that aren't nice.

What 'Taking a Break' could be like for more people

We've met some people who are having a good time when they aren't with their families. They spend time with people and when they go away it's to have a good time. We met a man whose dad was very ill and the man who was his friend spent more time with him because he was sad. He stayed in Martin's house some nights and he stayed in Liverpool near his friends. We think this is good. We want to make friends near where we live.

Figure 2.5

Figure 2.5

We want people to get to know us and know the sorts of things we like doing. Sometimes it's nice to do things with someone who likes doing the same things.

Figure 2.6

Figure 2.7

We don't think respite places can get to know us well. If I got sent to a respite place, who would look after my dad? I'm a carer.

It would be much better if people got to know us properly by spending time with us. Sometimes they don't even know what food we like. To find out they could eat with us!

Figure 2.8

Reference

Flynn, M. with Liverpool Self Advocates (1994) *Taking a Break: Liverpool's Respite Services for Adult Citizens with Learning Disabilities*. Manchester: National Development Team.

Chapter 3

Short-Term Care
Parental Perspectives

Philippa Russell

This chapter draws heavily on the personal experiences of parents who have been in contact with the Council for Disabled Children and the National Development Team, both on an individual basis and at workshops. The personal circumstances of each family have been anonymised and their names, and certain other details, changed. Many parents said it was very hard to be open and honest with service providers about what were often very painful feelings. However, they felt it was very important that the wide range of feelings and concerns they experienced should be shared and discussed more widely.

Introduction

The past decade has seen major developments in terms of flexible family support systems which provide extra help to parents wanting to care for a child with a disability within their own home. Access to regular (and emergency) short-term care is invariably named as a key service in local authority reviews of parents' expectations of local services, but in most authorities demand frequently exceeds supply. The OPCS surveys (1989a, 1989b) noted the pressures on many parents' everyday lives, but the limited access which families had to short-term care. Historically short-term care developed as an *emergency* service. Parents used long-stay hospitals and other forms of institutional care in desperation and frequently with considerable guilt. Professionals often feared that regular use of short-term care might lead to 'abandonment' and child care was not seen as the key issue. The concept of 'respite care' paralleled the notion of 'asylum', invariably within an institution, for vulnerable people. Many parents rejected such support because they could not accept the labels and the associated stigma. But

35

in the past decade, short-term care has increasingly been seen as one aspect of an integrated support system for families with a wide range of children with special needs. Parents equally have higher expectations of the location, availability and quality of the service offered.

The Children Act 1989, which applies in its entirety only to England and Wales, has had a major impact upon the *planning* and review of short-term care – many parents have welcomed the more pro-active assessment and planning arrangements for children 'looked after by the local authority' (Russell 1995). However, a range of unresolved issues exists within many current arrangements for short-term care about the provision of age-appropriate care, about emergency provision and, perhaps most importantly, about what parents actually feel about the whole process of needing and using short-term breaks. Social services departments' integration of 'children with disabilities' within the wider definition of 'children in need' has also caused difficulties for some families. Publicity about child protection issues has heightened sensitivity to possible connotations of inadequate parenting if a parent uses *any* social services provision. Anxiety about external perceptions of families using social services provision has in turn made many parents reluctant to agree to their child's name being placed on a local authority register of disabled children under Schedule 2 of the Children Act. However, without adequate information on the local population of children with disabilities and their families, the local authority is further disadvantaged in terms of creating services which are acceptable, accessible and user friendly, and in responding to the expectations arising from changing family structures. There are very different aspirations among new carers, many of whom are in paid employment, may be distant from traditional family networks and who furthermore expect the *best* for their children. They increasingly expect any provision to be integrated within mainstream children's services and avoid 'bussing' to distant segregated provision with the consequent loss of education and local leisure opportunities. Conversely, there are increasing numbers of children in the community with very complex and often degenerative disabilities and medical conditions for whom simplistic notions of 'integration' without appropriate specialist support will rapidly lead to failure to identify short-term carers, breakdowns of placements and anxious and unsupported parents.

Short-term care on its own is not a universal panacea. Stalker and Robinson (1991) found that 55 per cent of parents interviewed in

Croydon and 65 per cent of parents interviewed in Sheffield wanted other kinds of help apart from short-term care. The OPCS studies (1989a, 1989b) similarly showed that even when parents wanted short-term care, parents of younger children would have preferred it to be domiciliary (with carers coming to the family home), while other parents were prioritising sitting services, holiday play schemes and practical help such as aids and equipment.

All the recent surveys highlight a number of common themes with regard to *parents'* perspectives about short-term care and their priorities. In effect parents want:

- a local service, where the child can attend school as if he or she were living at home and the parents do not have long drives to and from the provision offered

- good quality child care which ensures that the child is neither treated as 'sick' nor regarded simplistically as needing no special support

- availability on demand

- better management of waiting lists and preparation for first placement – using short-term care for the first time can be stressful

- a service which meets the needs of all the children at different ages and stages and which recognises that some children will require very specialist support

- age-appropriate care (with no mixing of ages and with interesting and relevant activities for the children concerned)

- an integrated programme of family support

- information and choice

- a recognition that all family members are valuable and that parents should not need to justify the use of short-term care in order to enable siblings or parents to enjoy their own interests and activities

- services negotiated as part of a 'care package' with a clearly designated care manager.

Partnership with parents

'Motherhood has a single long-term goal, which could be described as a mother's eventual unemployment! A successful mother (or father) brings up their children to do without them. But if a child has a disability or special need, there may be no longer term unemployment. In effect, the "life plan" which all parents make for their children will be different for the child with disability or a special need. Some parents, particularly if they have low incomes, poor self-esteem, poor housing and little family support – may find the adjustment to disability too difficult to cope with. They are not bad parents. They do care. But somebody has to care for them as people before they can enter the wonderful new world of partnership between parents and professionals that we all hear so much about. Having a disabled child changes you for life!' (Parent attending a National Development Team workshop, Flynn and Russell 1991).

Being a parent (natural or substitute) of a disabled child can be a challenging experience and parental attitudes to short-term care will be directly affected by experiences in other areas of their lives. Philip and Duckworth (1982), in a review of studies of family life with a disabled child, commented that:

> 'Many families are not really coping, even though they are not breaking down. Rather they experience and meet their problems to the best of their abilities and often face secondary problems as a result. It is often the *accumulation* of these problems that disturbs relationships within the family and between family and society… in brief, research is now beginning to demonstrate that the real problem is not so much one of family pathology as one of how to give practical assistance to families while, at the same time, keeping in mind that the tasks they face are so difficult that only a few exceptional families can be expected to be fully equipped to undertake them without help from the outside.' (p.46)

Philp and Duckworth's observations are repeated in a later review of studies on the lives of families and disabled children (Baldwin and Carlisle 1994), which notes that *all* reviews and studies agree that there are four key criteria for supporting families (or other carers) of disabled children, namely:

- the availability of information on the child's disability and on the full range of support services

- recognition of the emotional and social context of assessment, and the anxiety and disappointment about the use of special provision and services for some families

- acknowledging the high degree of stress that some parents live under

- encouraging community support (particularly for parents and carers who find it difficult to access parent groups and community networks).

A major issue for local authorities providing services for 'looked after' disabled children will be the support which foster parents, short-term care services and any residential provision provide for *parents*. Short-term care is a unique and highly valued service, but many families find shared care very stressful until a close personal working relationship is established. Parents may also feel guilty that they cannot care for a child on a full-time basis and everybody has a major role in making parents feel confident and competent – and encouraging them to see shared care as a positive experience. Parents may be very anxious in planning for the initial placement. Some children will be medically frail; they may have poor communication skills and their parents will have had little experience of leaving them with other people. Creating partnerships, making parents feel comfortable and welcome (and able to be honest in their contributions to assessment) and recognising the unique and special knowledge they can contribute will be critical.

Research findings confirm the major changes in family life which can accompany the care of a disabled child. Glendinning (1983) found in a study for the Family Fund that out of 361 young children with disabilities, 50.1 per cent could not be left alone for even ten minutes in a day. Baldwin and Carlisle (1994), reviewing research on families with disabled children, comment that many parents are 'not really coping' and that families are frequently unaware of support services, or fear they may not be enough. Hubert (1991) notes one mother who said that when her son first used short-term care, she would 'pray he didn't die before I came to collect him'. Another parent related her desperation in having to use short-term care, despite her anxieties about the care of her severely disabled son. Her husband had insisted that they needed time together and she knew it was crucial for their marriage to 'take time out'. Other parents, however, have spoken passionately about 'real friendship', 'the pleasure of sharing small achievements' and 'the bliss of knowing there is someone who can help. She (the carer) is like my best friend' (Flynn and Russell 1991). In many instances increased family mobility, poverty, homelessness and single-parent status diminish the existing fragile networks of support, but research also suggests that there *are* ways of supporting families and that substitute carers may have an important role in restoring the natural parents' competence and confidence – or in maintaining family relationships when a child has to live away from home. OPCS (1989b) noted the worrying trend for children with disabilities living away from home to slip out of contact with their natural families and friends in their home community. The Children Act reminds all of us of the importance of these networks (which disabled children and young people are unlikely to sustain without support) and local authorities may wish to consider the role of the *independent visitor* as a means of maintaining family and community links, particularly when a child is placed at some distance from home.

A critical role in supporting *all* families caring for a disabled child is assessment of what the *family* thinks it needs. Russell notes that:

> 'Families with a disabled child frequently have less time, energy and income than other parents to get out and make local connections and find the support they want. Many lack a key worker to coordinate support. At a recent National Development Team Parents' Workshop, parents stressed the need for services to acknowledge the needs of all the children in a family (including the children of foster parents or short-term carers), to recognise that parents can make choices and to provide services which did not make parents feel like "crises" or "undeserving poor". One parent said in bewilderment, "all I wanted was a good childminder twice a week, but I had to go on a waiting list; I was given a residential short-term care place to cover a part-time job. I felt they worried that I couldn't care for my child. It seemed so expensive and complicated – like the 17 different professionals who theoretically plan for my child's needs!"' (1994, p.23)

Russell went on to note that services for parents (and children) should:

- build upon what parents and families already know
- provide user-friendly assessment systems (for example through the use of diaries, videos, etc.)

- recognise that parents can be trainers – for family placements, residential care
- avoid blame and acknowledge that some children present major challenges to everyday life
- recognise the pain and loss which accompanies diagnosis and assessment, however carefully carried out
- create positive partnerships between parents and service providers (recognising that many parents find it very difficult to cope with the care of a disabled child living away from home and will be sensitive to any real or implied criticism about their ability to cope)
- recognise that children are part of families and that fathers, siblings and the extended family have a role to play.

The Social Services Inspectorate (1994), in their report of the first national inspection of services for disabled children, propose that short-term placements should be arranged by the local authority as part of a package of services where a disabled child or the parent/carers are assessed as in need of this service and note that short-term placements should provide good quality child care which is local, trusted, meets complex needs, is culturally compatible, age appropriate, and integrated into wider services. The inspectorate saw 'partnership with parents' as the cornerstone of an effective short-term care service. In practice parents have variable experiences of short-term care as a component in a wider range of support. Geall (1991), in *Sharing the Caring*, identified a number of key concerns for partnership with parents which have been mirrored in other studies, namely the importance of:

- a good level of physical and emotional care
- the need for services to be accessible
- a homely environment which is fun for the child
- continuity of care
- getting a service before the first crisis
- information and choice
- flexibility
- a recognition of the need to have time for yourself and other children

- real partnership with parents and a recognition of the real pressures in their everyday lives
- short-term breaks not being treated as a universal panacea but as part of a menu of services.

Geall, like Baldwin and Carlisle (1994), recognises the high levels of stress experienced by many families and notes the connection between stress and inadequate support at periods of transition. Baldwin and Carlisle comment that:

> 'The need for information and advice and counselling is ongoing, but becomes more crucial at critical transition periods. These may be transitions and changes in the condition or commonly accepted developmental mile-stones often accompanied by changes in statutory provision... information needs to encompass the condition itself, its prognosis and practical management, the remit of and help available from statutory and voluntary sector sources, the benefit system and so on.' (1994, p.41)

Using short-term care for the first time is a transition time in itself. Transitions in sharing care may also be accompanied by changes in a child's disability or medical condition. 'Tina', describing her experiences with an adopted child from Eastern Europe who has HIV and is beginning to be unwell, comments that:

> 'The first thing was the diagnosis she was HIV – I didn't really take that in, she seemed perfectly well. Then she wasn't so well but I put it down to her early childhood, orphanage etc. They persuaded me to use a link family scheme in my area... I didn't really want *anyone* to take her, I thought she would feel she was being abandoned yet again. But it worked and then the real change came. She got AIDS and she really started to go downhill. But my link worker was marvellous. She said to me: it's like a second bereavement, and I know what she means. I do now need a break. "Sadie" is often ill. I can't leave her with anyone. And almost the best thing is that her carers are the friends I really need. They know her health status and it doesn't upset them. I can talk to them and they'll understand how dreadful I feel. I want to be strong for Sadie; I know she will die. I don't think I could cope without any shared care. It's like an extra family that doesn't judge you. I call it real "shared care".' (personal communication)

Tina's experience – and her recognition that good-quality short-term care supports the carer as well as the child – will be recognised by many parents.

Her views are mirrored in those of parents discussing short-term care at a parents' workshop (Russell 1994). Asked to give key messages to social services departments setting up new short-term care schemes, the parents stated clearly what they wanted:

- A local friend, like one of the family, to give us a hand. I want her to be local, because then 'David' can go to school, see the same people and I don't have to get on to a motorway at 6 pm on a Friday evening and trek across half a county...

- Somewhere where she is really *wanted* with no half suppressed sighs on the end of the phone when I ring, somewhere which is fun for her too...

- Anything, really anything, that would give us a break – Thomas is so difficult that no one wants him. Sometimes I think I'll ring the NSPCC and say I'm about to kill him. But would *they* do anything once they see what he's like? Excluded from school, from play-schemes, from everywhere, I can't see any alternative to 52 weeks boarding if we don't get some help soon.

- Laura's only three – she was a 'prem' baby and really there's everything wrong with her. She needs a lot of care – I feel safer with a doctor and a nurse around. I don't see this so-called 'social care' as safe enough. We take her to a children's hospice now, it's a 300 mile round trip but we know she's *safe*. She's very little to go away, but honestly I can't cope without the break...

- Marcus is 17 now – he used to stay with a local family, go to the football on Saturday, just an ordinary life really: now he's too big and too old. We've been offered a place in a residential home, but honestly it's no home. What Marcus wants is a natural break with some fun just like his siblings.

- What gets me is the new charging policy – don't I save the local authority enough by coping most of the time? Can't I apply to be Tom's family link person?

- I don't really need short-term care – but I do need a childminder. But what I'm offered is a bed for two nights a week. It's a sledge-hammer hitting a nut!

Assessing need

Notwithstanding the commitment of the Children Act 1989 to the principle of 'partnership with parents' and a greater awareness across health, education and social services of the importance of developing user-friendly assessment procedures, most parents find assessment a daunting exercise. The Audit Commission, in *Seen but not Heard* (1994), found that only 25 per cent of parents felt that assessment arrangements were well co-ordinated. The SSI (1994), in their report of the first national inspection of services for children with disabilities, noted that social services departments needed to develop partnerships in the key area of 'recognising the emotional and personal needs of parents at the time of identification and assessment' (section 5.2.6) and that they (the inspectors):

> 'were concerned to find that services were not being provided to disabled children on the basis of clear and thorough assessments. Where assessments had taken place, they tended to be specifically to assess for one aspect of a service and were so under-stated that parents were frequently unaware that an assessment had taken place. Parents required more information about the process of assessment... it was sometimes unclear who had responsibility for implementing and reviewing plans when assessments had been made and there seemed to be a need for a clear model of care management to be adopted.' (5.9.8)

Most of the literature on short-term care reiterates the problems of assessment. Several studies (Robinson 1986, Stalker 1990, Hubert 1991, Geall 1991) remind us that actually negotiating a break can be stressful to families who have heavily invested in caring. One mother in the Honeylands evaluation (Brimblecombe and Russell 1988) commented that 'He [Dr Brimblecombe] always stressed that we didn't need a special reason for having a break. He wanted us to do the things we would have done if we hadn't been carers – going to the pub, shopping anything. He would say, "you don't need excuses here".' Another parent said that in her previous local authority:

> 'We always felt we had to use special pleading, we were made to feel guilty, frankly, because it was implied there were people who needed the service more than we did. That's a horrid feeling, feeling guilty when you're so tired anyway. Most of my friends,

they were always going to so-called funerals. No-one would dare ask if your friend or relative had *really* died!'

Some parents were very conscious that local authorities had a hard time 'rationing services'. One mother suggested that:

'Parents need to be up-front about why they want short-term care. It will be different in every case. Some families have good natural support systems, lots of friends and relatives. We didn't, no-one anywhere near and it got very hard. I started using it just a little at first to get some time for myself. I thought that helped my daughter too. If she hadn't been disabled, I would still have looked for some "natural breaks".'

Using the short-term break – some issues for parents

Several parents felt that justifying the use of short-term care presented challenges. One mother commented that she 'didn't know what to do with the time'. Another said she felt frightened that if she 'went back to doing what I used to do, well then I don't think I could start up again caring like this'. Several parents noted that using the time profitably required practice – some families would have lost touch with friends and occupations. She felt local authorities should encourage parents to 'practise' separation – 'not anything grand, just having a few hours away every now and again. Why not? Perhaps our children need to practise doing without us too.'

But practising 'doing without us' can be a painful process. 'Callum's' mother (in Hubert 1991) noted her personal stress in using a residential short-term care home which she definitely felt was inadequate for her son's needs. She describes how her son comes home clearly on heavy medication, in the wrong clothes and sometimes very distressed at having been away from home. She recalls her terrible fear that Callum might actually die while he is away; she 'prays for him every night'. But like many other families, she is also aware that her husband and the rest of the family need time too. Caring for Callum at home may have 'conditions' for the rest of the family. Callum's mother uses the time to please her family – and to acknowledge that they too have needs and wishes. However, it is a stressful and unrewarding time, with the knowledge that Callum's return will mark a 'rehabilitation' period of dealing with his neglect, misplaced clothes and his unhappiness at being away where he was not really wanted or cherished.

However, time away can be positive too. A parent using a flexible family placement scheme described how she found her carer to be:

> 'Wonderful, willing to work along with my arrangements, very encouraging to me to take up interests and activities that I'd given up years ago. I think we all gain from my new interests – and it's wonderful to know that "Amy" is so well looked after. I'm not ashamed to say that I use short-term breaks to have fun. I think Amy has fun too. We're better for the break.'

The focus in short-term care in recent years has rightly been upon *planned* short-term breaks, integrated within a wider programme of family support. But in practice family life may not be so well organised. 'Emily', at a workshop in the south east, commented that:

> 'The hardest thing is when you need help as an emergency. I am sorry to say that for us local parents, the final closure of... Hospital will be an utter disaster. We don't like it. To be honest we hate using it. Last time, I sat in the car in the drive and cried when I'd left him. But they are always there. My father had a heart attack; we knew he would probably die. I had to go 100 miles immediately and no-one would have my son. Eventually it was agreed I could book him into a small residential home he had used before. Then they wasted my time going through the whole booking process as if he had never been away from home before. Ten pages of forms, and they had them already, what he ate, what he drank, what his routine was. I feel ashamed of myself but as I went off, I said "If we'd been much longer, I would have been going to my father's funeral". I do wonder what they would have done if I'd had a road accident? Would they have got the ambulance to drive me round to fill all these wretched forms in first?'

The same parent acknowledged that social services departments have statutory duties to protect children. Her message was that:

> 'Short-term care should be seen as part of a whole "package" of services. If they know you, if they have assessed you, the package should be flexible. Emergencies do happen... I have known parents ask for residential education simply to get reliable cover for emergencies. Not everyone has a family, or friends, who will cope.

Really emergency care is not the same as a "short-term break" – I
know of one family whose child was sent off to a private home 300
miles away. His mother was in hospital and the poor child was at
the other end of the country. That's confusing short-term with
family care – what they needed was someone to help out in the
home, *not* a "red star" parcel service to remove the child.'

Another parent commented that it was 'so humiliating to have to break
down to get a service, sometimes you have to be an emergency to get
anything and then it is too late... if I had a link family scheme, I think I
would have coped. It was having nobody which was so hard.' The same
parent felt that she could not ask for a break when she had no real
reason for it:

'Just doing something *you* want, is not a reason for a short-term
break is it? What I needed was just to be *me* for a time. I love my
child, but I feel I have just become "mother", not any mother, *her*
mother... it's as if I never played the piano, had three other children, am a marvel with a paintbrush and roller! If you cease to be
anything but "mother", then you lose touch with reality. And
really children want you to be mother *and* something else as well,
don't they?'

Sometimes the effort of using short-term care negated its purpose.
'Sally', a working single parent with a very active child of nine, describes her feelings about accessing a service.

'To begin with, I found it really hard doing the booking. I *know* lots
of parents like being their own "manager", but I feel really uncomfortable. "Marge", our first carer, couldn't take "Tracey" the first
time I rang. She really couldn't. I know it wasn't an excuse, but at
the time I thought, well – that's that, I'm not being humiliated
about asking again. So I didn't ask her. Then I heard from my social
worker that Marge had been really upset, thought she's offended
me. She nearly stopped offering to be a link family. Really we all
needed more of an introduction – and I was so tired and so guilty,
I didn't think honestly that anyone would want to look after
Tracey.'

Another parent had been offered short-term care on three occasions but reflected that:

> 'I really didn't have the time to go through the assessment and planning bits of the system... I know they are right, but when you're exhausted, it didn't seem worth it. Anyway, I don't know they would have taken my child – he's big and he's difficult. I couldn't see him in a nice bedroom, all Laura Ashley and sprigged muslin curtains. But then I can't bear the thought of him in a big bare room either. What really worries me is if anything happens to me – I know my husband would like to start using short-term care immediately. But he doesn't live with David like I do.'

A third parent at the same parent workshop expressed her anger at 'short-term breaks that aren't breaks at all'. Her health authority was in dispute with the social services department about who should provide any nursing or specialist medical care when children used a small staffed group home for short-term breaks. Her daughter required both rectal diazepam and intermittent catheterisation. She had been 'trained' to provide both, but the local and health authorities could not agree about the insurance (and liability) of the paid care staff to acquire and administer the skills to provide the treatment. 'Susan' was therefore obliged to drive to the group home from her own house sometimes three or four times a day if help was required. The health authority had offered to provide the service but demanded payment. The neighbouring health authority had a totally different policy and automatically provided a community nurse to provide outreach care in a social-care setting. Susan felt that the effort, disruption to her and her child and the time involved in providing such care, totally distorted the idea of a 'natural break'. As she succinctly expressed it, 'the purpose of the break is supposed to be relieving me of this additional care – not going half round the country to provide it!'

Accessing short-term care – children with disabilities from ethnic minorities

> 'Raffique's parents do not like the idea of giving their child to anyone else, because they think they should care for him without anyone else's help. However, because their son has severe behavioural problems in addition to his physical handicap and learning

disability, he is difficult to control and his parents need a break. Initially his father was very reluctant to send Raffique to short-term care, because he thought his dietary needs could not be met. Social workers arranged for Halal food to be provided and now Raffique attends a day centre one day a week. Sometimes he also stays over the weekend and arrangements are made accordingly.' (Shah 1992, p.36)

'Anil, who is 12 years old and suffers from severe learning diffi-culties and is physically disabled, has never had short-term care. He lives in an extended family and his parents have to provide much support and help for Anil with toiletting, carrying him up and down stairs and playing with him so that he doesn't feel depressed. They have never been told about either day or short-term care.' (Shah 1992, p.37)

Most studies of short-term breaks show significant under-use by par-ents from minority ethnic groups. Shah (1992), in a study of Asian families with disabled children, highlights the barriers that access to short-term care entails when a family comes from a different commu-nity. The families in her study frequently lacked information about services; poor interpretation and translation facilities meant that infor-mation, if given, was not always accurate or relevant. Assumptions about the role of the extended family and attitudes to disability in the Asian community were often inaccurate and parents frequently suf-fered double discrimination with regard to disability and race.

Shah comments that:

'Disability, whether it is physical, mental, sensory or auditory, is not prejudiced... It transcends all races, beliefs and cultures. It creates similarly profound emotional, practical and psychological experiences for all parents, whoever they are. Unfortunately, where Asian families are concerned, common sense about a valid generalisation of attitudes towards disability is lost in the mists of ignorance and perceived cultural differences.' (1992, p.21)

Shah goes on to comment on the case studies of Anil and Raffique (see above) and the assumptions that may be made about why parents may refuse a service and whether they would want such a service in the first place. She warns against a set of common (and false) assumptions about

Asian families which may prevent them from getting the help they need in using short-term care and other community services:

- *Language*: language difficulties may lead to Asian mothers appearing not to want to use services, when in reality they cannot understand information presented without interpreters or translations being available. The availability of interpreters and translation facilities is crucial.

- *Ideas*: It is often automatically assumed that Asian families will not wish to accept short-term care. 'They believe children should only be cared for within the family'.

- *Cultural differences*: professionals (and voluntary organisations) may not understand the significance of culture and lifestyles – or they may make inaccurate assumptions about what families want.

- *Shame and guilt*: there are often beliefs that Asian families feel special shame and guilt about the birth of a child with a disability. In fact their feelings are as complex and individual as those in any family.

- *Services won't fit*: all children with disabilities are unique and often insufficient time is given to considering whether Asian families would or could use services which are generally available for disabled children in the area.

Shah observes that Asian families with a disabled child are in most respects like other families trying to live with and care for a child who may need extra time, attention and who may change family life. However, she also reminds us of the importance of providing services within a community context, so that families are not isolated or discriminated against when using them. She warns against false assumptions that parents do not want the same range of practical help as other families and emphasises the importance of:

- access to professional interpreters and translators

- being patient and open-minded, not being afraid to ask families what they would like and how they can be helped

- observing gender issues and being respectful of different customs and wishes

- acknowledging that past (or present) experiences of racism may make families suspicious of 'white' organisations offering help

- recognising the strength of mutual support – parents' groups provide information, practical help and friendship, if families know about them

- acknowledging the knock-on effects of poor housing, economic and social disadvantage and family illness – sometimes a child's disability is not the main problem within a family

- observing religious and cultural events – we can all gain from celebrating diversity

- being willing to learn – many families from minority groups can establish good relationships with trained and supportive white professionals

- recognising that disability affects all families and that short-term care can have a positive role.

The Children Act 1989 reminds us of the importance of recognising race, religion and culture in planning services for children 'looked after' by the local authority. However, this may require vigorous planning and careful thought when the child also has a disability. Roy Griffiths, in drafting *Community Care: An Agenda for Action* (1988), had assumed that the new arrangements for community care, with individual assessments and 'care packages', would result in better trained staff and more culturally sensitive services. However, Shah's research suggests that there are major obstacles. Ghulam Abbas, in a report on services for Asian people with disabilities (Association of Metropolitan Authorities 1994), similarly notes that:

- Services are currently taken up by only a small percentage of Asian service users. Many potential users simply do not know that help is available.

- Some services have taken positive steps to include users from a range of cultures and backgrounds. Others have not.

- There are major difficulties in providing material (and personal advice) in an appropriate language. Within the Asian community alone, there are five major languages used in the UK.

- Dietary and religious needs are often not acknowledged.

As Abbas notes on issues relating to *equal* access opportunities to support services for disabled children, we need to look at all our procedures (in consultation with the relevant minority ethnic communities) to ensure they are free from cultural or linguistic bias. Many families (and children) will need trained interpreters, advocates or liaison workers to help them through 'the system'. We also need to encourage more carers from the full range of minority groups to consider offering short or longer term care for children with disabilities and special needs. The success of those short-term care schemes which have positively recruited, trained and supported black families reminds us of the value placed by all families on practical and appropriate support and the dangers of making stereotyped assumptions about the wishes and needs of families within an increasingly multicultural society.

Conclusion

The past few years have seen major developments in short-term care. First, there has been growing recognition that the notion of 'respite' is inadequate and indeed discriminatory in the light of growing evidence of the *positive* contribution of short-term care to family lives. All parents need breaks. All parents from time to time look to relatives or friends for support. The challenge for disabled children and their families has been to create the same patterns of support, which extend the experiences and enrich the lives of the children, while ensuring that parents are secure and comfortable with the care provided. There is growing evidence that many parents need active encouragement actually to use short-term care, that many families are still unaware of the possibility of accessing such a service and that black families in particular may be excluded because of misconceptions about the role of the extended family and because of lack of information and confidence in the quality of provision offered. It is clear that many parents still have very individual ideas of what they want and need. Family-link schemes offer more than care; in many instances they offer opportunities for friendships, for shared celebrations of achievements and for mutual support when times are difficult. But some families still feel that their children are 'too difficult' for anyone else to care for. Some are offered short-term care when their actual needs are simpler and linked primarily to sitting and daycare services.

However, as the parent of a nine-year-old child with a rare metabolic disease commented on the 'shared care' she experienced, as her child visibly deteriorated:

'Short-term care has been my life-line. They [the family-link carers] always make me feel they are there. Initially I felt bad about using them. I felt my parents would say – if they can cope, why can't you? But everybody knows now we need them. The best thing is that Sam loves them too. He needs a break from our constant anxiety, our sadness, our tiredness. *He* needs what my daughter calls "fresh wallpaper". Sometimes Jenny [the carer] and I speak every day – other times we may not see each other for three weeks or so. Last time Sammie went there, it wasn't for a break; they invited him to their silver wedding party. It was wonderful. I see him in the photos on the mantlepiece, and I think he's part of that family for ever... that's the hardest thing about having a disabled child, you often feel they are just shadows in someone's eyes. Sammie is a real person for Jenny and Ted and that makes me feel real too.'

References

Association of Metropolitan Authorities (1994) *Special Child, Special Services?* Child Care Paper 4. London: AMA.

Audit Commission (1994) *Seen but not Heard.* London: HMSO.

Baldwin, S. and Carlisle, J. (1994) *Social Support for Disabled Children and Their Families: A Review of the Literature.* Social Work Services Inspectorate. Edinburgh: HMSO.

Brimblecombe, F. and Russell, P. (1988) *Honeylands: Developing a Service for Families with Handicapped Children.* London: National Children's Bureau.

Flynn, M. and Russell, P. (1991) Report of Parent Workshop. National Development Team for People with Learning Disabilities. (Copies available from the Council for Disabled Children, 8 Wakley Street, London EC1V 7QE, on receipt of an sae.)

Geall, R. (1991) *Sharing the Caring: Respite Care in the UK for Families and Children with Disabilities.* London: National Children's Home.

Glendinning, C. (1983) *Unshared Care: Parents and Their Disabled Children.* London: Routledge and Kegan Paul.

Griffiths, R. (1988) *Community Care: An Agenda for Action.* London: HMSO.

Hubert, J. (1991) *Home-bound: Crisis in the Care of Young People with Severe Learning Disabilities.* London: King's Fund Centre/Blackwells.

Office of Population Censuses and Surveys (1989a) Smyth, M. Report 5. *Surveys of Disability in the UK: The Financial Circumstances of Families with Disabled Children.* London: HMSO.

Office of Population Censuses and Surveys (1989b) Meltzer, H., Smyth, M. and Robus, N. Report 6. *Disabled Children: Services, Transport and Education.* London: HMSO.

Philip, M. and Duckworth, D. (1982) *Children with Disabilities and Their Families: A Review of the Literature.* Windsor: NFER-Nelson.

Robinson, C. (1986) *Avon Short-term Respite Care Schemes, Evaluation Study: Final Report.* Department of Mental Health, University of Bristol.

Russell, P. (1994) 'Access to the system.' In P. Mittler and H. Mittler (eds) *Innovation in Family Support for People with Learning Disabilities.* Preston: Lisieux Hall.

Russell, P. (1995) *The Children Act 1989: Children and Young People with Learning Disabilities – Some Opportunities and Challenges.* London: National Development Team and National Children's Bureau.

Shah, R. (1992) *The Silent Minority: Children with Disabilities in Asian Families.* London: National Children's Bureau.

Social Services Inspectorate (1994) *Services to Disabled Children and their Families: Report of the National Inspection of Services to Disabled Children and their Families.* London: HMSO.

Stalker, K. (1990) *Share the Care: An Evaluation of a Family-based Respite Care Service.* London: Jessica Kingsley Publishers.

Stalker, K. and Robinson, C. (1991) *Out of Touch – The Non-Users of Respite Care Services.* Norah Fry Research Centre: University of Bristol.

Chapter 4

Costing Breaks and Opportunities

Ann Netten

The need for cost information

There continues to be a growing demand for information about the costs and cost effectiveness of community care services. The demand is for a wide variety of purposes including estimating service prices, costing the effect of demographic changes or new policies, examining the technical efficiency of services over time and evaluating the cost effectiveness of innovations. Knapp (1995) has classified this range of purposes into four broad groups of demand: practice, policy, accountability and research.

The demand for cost information in the field of services that provide short-term care and breaks for carers and users is particularly acute because this is an area in which there is generally a dearth of cost information and which is growing rapidly in response to changed arrangements as a result of the National Health Service and Community Care Act (1990). It is also an area in which traditional approaches to providing breaks for carers are being challenged and innovative approaches are being explored. The practice demands for costs information include the need for an understanding of the costs among those considering providing such services. Those concerned with policy need to set such information in the context of alternative approaches to providing support to service users and their carers. Those concerned with funding services need an understanding of the costs of provision when evaluating value for money. Those with limited resources considering different approaches need research-based information about the comparative cost effectiveness of different approaches.

This chapter focuses primarily on the use of costs in a research context and begins by outlining the theoretical background and basic principles of costs research, using four 'rules' of costing. The implications of these rules are then explored for the costing of services which provide breaks for carers and opportunities for users. Elsewhere in this volume the wide variety of services that fall under this umbrella heading has been demonstrated. This chapter will focus on services used by adults with learning disabilites, drawing in particular on a recent study of innovative approaches to providing breaks (Hayes *et al*. 1995; see also Chapter 10 of this volume). These services linked users to support workers, carers or befrienders for 'sessions' which included a wide variety of activities such as social occasions, trips out, sport, shopping, weekend breaks and overnight stays.

Theoretical background and basic principles

The economic concept of opportunity cost defines what should be measured and how, when estimating costs. The rationale behind using this approach is discussed in detail elsewhere (see Netten and Beecham 1993). Ideally the opportunity cost of a service represents the value of alternative uses of the resources tied up in the production of that service. The opportunity cost of a unit of service represents the value tied up in producing an additional or marginal unit in the long term. Thus, when estimating the cost of a session of daycare provided at a facility, it is relevant to include capital costs as, at the margin, a new facility may need to be constructed to accommodate an expanding service.

This provides a valuable starting point in the estimation of costs, but inherent in the theory and the variety of purposes for estimation is a central characteristic of economic cost: there is no one absolute figure which represents the cost of a service. How the cost is estimated depends on the purpose of the costing and the circumstances of the service. In the example above, of daycare, whether or not the costs incurred by users travelling to the centre are included would depend on whether the purpose of the costing was a full economic evaluation or a pricing exercise. The capital cost of the facility would depend on whether the service was expanding (implying the need for new buildings) or reducing (implying the need to sell off existing buildings).

The purpose and circumstances of estimation are usually clear when costing, enabling appropriate assumptions to be made based on theoretical principles. Further problems arise, in practice, however, in disentangling the actual information on which costs are based. Allen and Beecham (1993) describe an approach to this process which helps clarify the important stages of estimating costs in practice. This involves describing service elements, identifying the cost implications of these elements, identifying activities and calculating service units in order to calculate the total and unit cost of the service.

The process of estimation has implications for the way in which cost information can and should be used. Integrating these issues, Knapp (1993) has identified the basic principles of applied costs research, summarised in four 'rules':

- costs should be comprehensively measured
- when comparisons are made, only 'like-with-like' comparisons have full validity
- cost variations that inevitably arise in an empirical exercise should be explored and exploited
- cost information should be integrated with information on user and other outcomes.

The following sections consider each of these rules in turn, with specific reference to the estimation of costs of short-term care services.

Comprehensive costs

Ensuring that costs are measured comprehensively is important for validity in analyses made and inferences drawn. For example, if a comparison is to be made between providing support to people in private households and the costs of residential care, it is essential that accommodation expenses are included in the costs of the care package of people in private households as these are included in the costs of residential care. Special care needs to be taken when considering indirect costs, which are often difficult to establish and to measure, as inappropriate conclusions can be drawn if important costs are ignored. This is particularly the case with innovative services which often draw on the unpaid time of professional staff. If the cost of such time is ignored, then a service can appear to be relatively cheap to run. This may result both in underfunding and unrealistic expectations in terms of effectiveness when the service is introduced into mainstream provision.

It is not a straightforward task to ensure comprehensive costing even when this is limited to specific services. Previous work on costing services which provide breaks for carers has tended to focus on the budgeted costs of running schemes (for example, Robinson 1986, Orlik *et al.* 1991). The problems associated with this are acknowledged by the authors of such research, but this still leaves users of the information unclear about the cost implications, should they wish to introduce such a scheme, and unable to compare costs with alternative ways of providing a similar service.

Annual costs 199?/?	Value	Comments
Co-ordinator/organiser salaries		
Salary oncosts		
Worker/volunteer payments		
Expenses		
Equipment (e.g. sports equipment)		
Training		
Transport expenses		
Vehicles		
Direct rev overheads:		
management		
secretarial/clerical		
travel – (staff mileage)		
postage/photocopying		
heating/lighting		
telephone		
insurance		
Indirect rev overheads (e.g. personnel/finance)		
Capital overheads:		
office space		
office equipment		
Unit estimation		
Number of clients		
Number of clients with challenging behaviours/multiple disabilities		
Number of sessions/hours per year		
Type of session (e.g. one-to-one)		
Length of sessions		
Occupancy		
Unit costs (per client per year, per hour, per session)		

Figure 4.1. Worksheet for estimating cost of services providing flexible respite service

One way to address the problem of ensuring comprehensiveness in estimating costs is illustrated in Figure 4.1. Although there was considerable variation in the services delivered in a study of innovative approaches to short-term care (Hayes *et al.* 1995), both within and between individual schemes, from a costing perspective there were common patterns. For example, common across the schemes was the role of organisers or co-ordinators responsible in most services for ensuring (among other duties) that each user was linked to an individual worker or volunteer. These patterns allowed the development of a worksheet based on the approach described by Allen and Beecham (1993) and the schemata used in Netten (1994a).[1] The top half of the worksheet identifies the different elements of this type of service, helping to ensure that each element is checked when estimating costs and any lack of information is noted. Lack of information about a particular element identifies where assumptions about costs need to be made and allows consultation across schemes to enable appropriate assumptions to be made. Netten (1994b) describes the methodology and assumptions used in more detail.

The information about the type of service provided in the lower half of the worksheet feeds into the estimation of the unit cost of the service and facilitates analysis of the type of service being provided. Information about the type and level of service receipt is important in services that provide breaks, as by their very nature they are intermittent and of varying lengths, even within schemes.

When services are being costed for the purposes of estimating the costs of a care package, it is necessary to be clear about the cost effects of receiving a service. These may be to the user or carer; for example, the costs incurred by either in getting to and from the location of the service. To establish this the data needed includes private costs such as fares for public transport but excludes charges for transport provided by the service. For research purposes it is important to establish the gross costs of a service to all parties avoiding double counting (so excluding charges for services). While it may be of interest to analyse who bears how much of the cost, the issue of how much users and carers are charged for services providing breaks is separate from the issue of the costs of the provision.

---

1 A similar approach is being developed by Dickey, Latimer, Beecham and Powers (1994).

There may also be implications for the costs to other service providers. For example, when the break takes the form of a short-term residential placement, this may have an impact on the costs of regularly provided services such as daycare or home-care assistance. It is necessary to establish whether there is any saving in practice for those services while the user is in the residential placement, in order to cost accurately the package of care. It is also important to ensure that the costing is measured over a period of time that adequately reflects the use of short-term care services. The issue of what unit to cost over what period is also important when considering comparing services.

Comparing like with like

Identifying the costs of a limited number of services, each of which has the provision of breaks for carers as a primary objective, invites the process of comparison. Ensuring that like is compared with like is particularly difficult to do in the types of service included in the study by Hayes *et al.* (1995), because the linking theme was simply innovative approaches to providing short-term care. In practice the schemes were dominated by two of five types of respite service that can be distinguished in terms of their cost implications. Two types of service provide *short-term residential* care: *family based* and *facility based*. *Facility-based daycare* is the most widespread traditional type of service that provides regular daycare in one location. More innovative services focus on taking users to a variety of venues, usually for periods of a few hours. While these trips and outings can include overnight stays, weekend breaks and even holidays the service is providing an activity rather than a different location for care. For the purposes of this chapter this type of service is termed *activity based*. Other respite services could be categorised as primarily *sitting* services, as the support worker stays with the user in the user's home, allowing carers to go out. Again this could be overnight or for weekend breaks, but the location is the carer and user's home.

The majority of schemes in the study (listed in Table 4.1) provided activity-based services which involved individual befrienders or supporters taking users out on trips, to educational or social events or helping with practical tasks such as shopping. Each 'session' lasted a few hours and its format depended on the needs of the user and the relationship he or she built up with the support worker. Schemes D and

G are the only services that do not provide a one-to-one support service for all users. In scheme D some of the sessions, including a regular Saturday 'club', link two or three users to each support worker. About a quarter of the hours provided in total are on a one-to-one basis. Scheme G at present provides only group activities such as canoeing and sailing trips, outings, and visits to the cinema. Schemes A, B and C provided weekend breaks in addition to such outings, with scheme A focusing on particularly 'difficult to care for' users. The types of session provided by scheme F include sitting, in addition to taking users out. Only one of the schemes reported here, scheme H, provided a family-based short-term residential service.

Table 4.1. Estimated costs of the schemes

		Average unit cost per user (1993/94)		
Scheme	No. of users	£ per year	£ per average session	£ per hour
A	18	15,273	£102 per session	34
			£1629 per weekend	
B	20	5206	£60 per session	15
C	73	1342	£65 per session	12
D	29	1549	£49 per session	11
E	26	936	£23 per session	6
F	91	841	£71 per session	18
G	78	335	£38 per session	7
H	25	1604	£118 per overnight stay	5

An important first step when comparing the costs of this type of service is considering the unit to be costed. One objective the schemes have in common, regardless of whether they are short-term residential, activity-based or sitting, is to provide a break for carers and users. The costs of providing a source of such breaks over a year for a user and his/her carer is one way to conceptualise a unit cost, as is the cost of each 'break' or session. As these sessions vary from weekends and holidays to a few hours in the pub, it is also useful to include the cost of an hour's provision. Taken together, these give a helpful picture of what is provided, how much and at what cost. For example, in Table 4.1 the comparison of costs of different units gives an insight into the intensity with which breaks are provided. Schemes C and F have similar hourly and sessional costs but the level of provision per user is such that average annual costs per user for scheme C are more than double the costs of scheme F. Clearly scheme F provides a less intensive service than scheme C.

Another consideration is the range of costs per user within each scheme. These varied considerably depending on the type of service. Scheme A, a health authority-based scheme in an early stage of development, was costed on the basis of a standard package for each user: two three-hour sessions each week and four weekend breaks each year. Scheme C provided a wide range of support, from linked carers who provided a few hours occasionally in an emergency, to providing one user with two sessions of more than 12 hours every week. Robinson (1986), in an analysis of a single scheme, explored the implications of this, categorising costs as fixed (required to administer the scheme) and variable (related to direct provision). It was not possible to define costs consistently in this way across the schemes reported here. This was due in part to the early stage of development of the schemes, but also reflected the variation in the way that direct provision was organised. Some schemes paid workers on a sessional basis, making identification of the variable element of costs clear. In other cases the allocation of costs to fixed and variable aspects of the schemes was much less obvious.

Considering the degree to which schemes are providing similar services is an important first step before comparing costs. It was identified above that there are five main types of service: family-based residential, facility-based residential, facility-based daycare, activity-based sessions, and sitting. The costs of both types of residential service necessarily include living expenses and will normally extend over longer periods, including night-time, when there will normally be no active input from carers. Thus, while the costs of sessions would be expected to be higher than facility-based daycare, activity-based schemes and sitting services, hourly costs would be expected to be lower. The expectation would also be that facility-based day care and activity-based schemes would incur more direct expenses for transport, hire of equipment and entry fees than sitting services. Clearly, services which are facility based, be they daycare or residential, would incur higher fixed capital costs than other services. Such services have not been discussed further here as the study focused on non-facility-based schemes.

The costs of the family-based short-term residential scheme (scheme H) are lower than the majority of the other, primarily activity-based schemes, on an hourly basis. If the costs are compared to facility-based residential care, however, the average weekly cost of £826 is more than double that reported for long-term local authority residential care (Netten 1994a). The direct fees to carers of £232 per occupied bed per week in the respite scheme were very similar to the direct revenue costs of a local authority bed. The main difference lay in the level of overheads. Netten (1994a) has made no allowance for managing agency overheads in the estimate of the costs of local authority residential care, although it is unlikely that these would be very high. Work by the Audit Commission (1993) suggests that the local authority managing agency overhead costs adds about 5 per cent to the costs of residential care for older people. It would be expected that short-term care would carry much higher levels of overhead cost associated with the organisation of the breaks. When the further complication is added of finding and matching carers to users, it is not surprising that overhead costs should dominate the costs of the short-term family-based residential service.

There are other issues that need to be taken into consideration when ensuring that like is being compared with like. For example, are the services being provided for a similar clientele? It would be expected that services catering for people with challenging behaviours would be costlier to fund than for those without. Once it has been established that there is a basic similarity in the service provided, it is important to explore such reasons for variations in costs.

Exploring cost variations

Analysing the reasons for variations in costs can give a useful insight into the operation of services and what can be expected of innovations if they are to be introduced more widely. The best context for this is a large-scale study that allows the use of the cost function approach to unpick the causes of variation and the effects of different factors on the costs of provision (Knapp 1993). In the type of study reported here, this is not possible. Nevertheless it is of interest to examine the costs of these few schemes to consider whether any useful conclusions can be drawn for those considering purchasing or providing such services.

Although comparisons clearly need to be made with caution, there is sufficient similarity in what the bulk of the schemes are providing for it to be useful to investigate variations in costs between the schemes. Hourly costs give a consistent basis for comparison, although it has been identified above that scheme H is not directly comparable with the other schemes in Table 5.1. Four of the schemes (B, C, D and F) have hourly costs which lie within the range of £11 to £18 per hour. Of the three remaining schemes, E and G have much lower costs per hour than the others and scheme A is notably more expensive. What conclusions can be drawn about the reasons for this pattern of variation?

The expected reasons for variations in costs of services include estimation issues, differences in intermediate outputs, characteristics of users, characteristics of staff, and providing sector (Netten 1994a). These are discussed below. It should be noted, however, that with such small numbers of schemes the discussion about variations in costs can only be speculative.

Estimation issues

It is likely that problems associated with estimation may account for some variations, and some *absence* of variation reported. To take the latter case first, where actual estimates have not been available, assumptions have been based on the evidence of other schemes or at least on a consistent basis. Necessarily, such estimates do not reflect actual variations in cost. Problems in establishing accurate costs are particularly acute in newly established and rapidly expanding services. Adjustments need to be made to reflect a reasonably stable picture but which also link what was provided with the costs incurred.

There is also the issue of apparent variations reflecting problems in estimation. In this study the estimates that were available for scheme E were considered underestimates by those providing them, but they were the best available. It is probable, therefore, that the costs reported for this scheme are underestimates of the true costs of providing such a service. Similarly, the costs reported for scheme A are based on estimates rather than actual expenditure and may overestimate the costs of providing the service. Nevertheless, although the range may be exaggerated, there does appear to be some genuine underlying variation which it is of interest to pursue.

Intermediate outputs

Intermediate outputs are indicators of what it is the service is providing. These are distinct from final outputs which are the benefits derived by the users and their carers. The variation in these has been discussed above to some extent, when considering whether 'like' was being compared with 'like'. The range of intermediate output for this kind of service would include the types of session, flexibility of provision, quality of care and the activities provided. For the most part the sessions were provided on a one-to-one basis. The only evidence of differences in intermediate outputs that can be deduced from the information available in the costing exercise were related to schemes G, D and H. It has been identified above that scheme H provided a residential service, so it would be expected that sessional costs would be higher and hourly costs lower than a peripatetic service. Scheme G differed from the other services in that the emphasis was on introducing users to activities and fostering independence rather than linking users to particular workers. All the sessions in this scheme were for groups of between six and ten users with a few volunteers attached to each group. Similarly, scheme D linked more than one user to each support worker, providing a minority of sessions on a one-to-one basis. These last two schemes did have the lower hourly costs that would be expected as a result of the lower staff to user ratios.

Characteristics of users

It has been noted above that with such a small number of schemes it is difficult to distinguish individual factors that affect costs. This is particularly true when considering the impact of user characteristics. Most services were provided on a one-to-one basis and among these there was no clear association between hourly costs and the proportion of users with challenging behaviours and multiple disabilities. This is not surprising. Although there will be users for whom there is a need to have more than one support worker, these very high staffing ratios mean that a wide range of characteristics can be accommodated at very similar costs. Differences are evident at the extremes, however. It was noticeable, for example, that scheme E, with the lowest hourly costs,

was the only scheme that had no users with challenging behaviours
and multiple disabilities.

The most notable link between user characteristics and costs was
evident in scheme A which catered solely for people with very high
levels of disability and challenging behaviours. The effects of focusing
on such users were reflected in both higher staffing levels and the skills
and experience of the support workers. In contrast to the other
schemes, nursing staff provided one-to-one support for a particularly
difficult to care for group of users. If the users could not be cared for as
well by less well-qualified staff, then the reason for the higher costs is
the higher dependency level of the users, not the characteristics of staff.
Characteristics of staff can have a separate impact on costs, however.

Characteristics of staff

The support workers directly providing these services included salaried and waged workers and volunteers paid on a sessional basis. As
would be expected, the costs of co-ordination and training were pro-
portionately higher in those services where direct provision was dominated by volunteers. Thus, the use of volunteers did not necessarily
result in lower unit costs, although the schemes with the lowest hourly
cost (schemes E and G) were provided entirely by unpaid volunteers
building on pre-existing links with volunteers, befrienders or adult
placement services. Cost restraint was not a primary purpose of using
volunteers for this type of scheme, however. One objective of many
schemes was to increase links between users and their local communities, expanding their social and support networks. Volunteers from the
local area involving users in community activities provided a useful
approach to this objective.

Providing sector

Historically, health-authority based services have been more expensive
than local authority provision, which in turn has been more costly than
services provided by the independent sector (Netten 1994a). This clear
distinction was not evident here, however. The innovative nature of
the schemes in the current cost-conscious climate was one reason for
this. In several cases the expectation was that the services, having been
initiated by local authorities, and in one case an NHS trust, would
become free standing and self-financing, providing value for money
for the purchasing authority. Services developed by non-profit organ-

isations similarly needed to demonstrate value for money to purchasing authorities. Although the focus of most schemes was on demonstrating the value of their activities, necessarily the development in both types of setting was operating on the margins, scraping up resources wherever possible, but acutely aware of the limitations of those resources. Structural differences did remain, however. For example, non-profit organisations were much more likely not to pay employers' superannuation contributions for salaried and waged staff.

Clearly, with so few schemes, the discussion about reasons for variation (or lack of variation) in costs must be speculative. However, the main constraint in the discussion is lack of information about outcomes.

Outcomes

The objective when providing care is the benefit or welfare of the user and carer. The nature of the study reported here meant there was no information about such outcomes: indeed there appears to be a general dearth of studies which link costs of short-term care services to outcomes for users and carers. Cambridge *et al.* (1994) report on costs and outcomes for people with learning difficulties five years after being discharged from hospital, but very few of these used 'respite' services. Orlik *et al.* (1991) describe a wide variety of family-based schemes for people with learning difficulties including some information about costs but do not look at the outcomes for users and carers. Levin, Moriarty and Gorbach (1994) analysed a range of services providing breaks for carers of older people with dementia and follow up the outcomes, but do not link these to costs. The only study which specifically linked outcomes of short-break services (for children with learning difficulties and their carers) to costs (Gerard 1990) was limited to five schemes, making it difficult to draw any robust conclusions. Discussing the difficulties associated with linking costs and outcomes for 'respite' care, Gerard identifies the problems of comparing like-with-like, lack of validated and reliable instrumentation for evaluating the impact of services on informal carers, and the endemic problem of a small number of observations for any specialist service.

The lack of information about costs and outcomes of short-term care across client groups is an important omission. While there is a widespread concern with establishing value for money, there does not appear to be an equivalent level of activity directed towards finding what benefits are gained from these services at what cost. It is not appropriate to address here the issue of benefits for users and their carers and how these should be measured. It is relevant, however, to note that some of the supposed benefits have cost implications. For example, in the field of care of older people, there is often an assumption that access to services that provide breaks will reduce the likelihood of carer breakdown and thus the admission to residential care, although this was not the finding of Levin *et al.* (1994). Their findings did suggest, however, that there was a role for such services in supporting long-term carers. Clearly any analysis that wishes to explore the cost implications of services providing breaks needs to set these in the context of the needs of the individual users and carers, the whole package of care received and over a sufficiently long period to be able to explore the cost and outcome implications for both users and carers of different patterns of care over time.

Conclusion

This chapter began by identifying the need for cost information in the growing field of short-term care provision. The focus has been on services for people with learning difficulties and their carers, but the need for such information is not confined to this particular group. It has been possible to draw on one study which was concerned with innovative, flexible services and to describe a comprehensive approach to costing these services.

The importance of comparing like-with-like and exploring cost variations has been emphasised and five types of service (family-based short-term residential, facility-based short-term residential, facility-based daycare, activity-based and sitting) have been identified, which have different cost implications. However, there are limits to what is possible in the context of small-scale studies. Larger scale studies using multivariate analyses allow the unpicking of inter-related effects. For example, it has been hypothesised above that sitting schemes would be less costly than an activity-based scheme. No conclusions can be drawn from the lack of any evidence of lower costs in the scheme which provided sitting as part of its range of services, as it is not possible here to consider the impact of cost-raising factors, such as quality of care and flexibility of provision.

However, the main problem associated with drawing conclusions about the costs of these services is the lack of information about outcomes (Gerard 1990). The study reported here was focusing on identifying innovative and interesting approaches to providing breaks for carers and opportunities for people with learning difficulties. This is an important first step. However, if those responsible for purchasing and providing such services are to target their resources and efforts in the way that best achieves value for money, they need information about the cost effectiveness of these schemes. The current focus on community-based care and support for carers is resulting in a growth of short-term care. The cost effectiveness of such services should be a priority for future research.

References

Allen, C. and Beecham, J. (1993) 'Costing services: Ideals and reality.' In A. Netten and J. Beecham (eds) *Costing Community Care: Theory and Practice*. Aldershot: Ashgate.

Audit Commission (1993) *Taking Care: Progress with Care in the Community*. London: Audit Commission.

Cambridge, P., Hayes, L. and Knapp, M. with Gould, E. and Fenyo, F. (1994) *Care in the Community – Five Years On: Life in the Community for People with Learning Disabilities*. Personal Social Services Research Unit, University of Kent, Canterbury. Aldershot: Ashgate.

Dickey, B., Latimer, L., Beecham, J. and Powers, K. (1994) *Toolkit for Estimating Per Unit Mental Health Program Costs*. The Evaluation Center, HSRI, Cambridge, MA 02140.

Acknowledgements

This chapter feeds into a project supported by the Joseph Rowntree Foundation as part of its programme of research and innovative development projects, which it hopes will be of value to policy makers and practitioners. The facts presented and views expressed in this chapter, however, are those of the author and not necessarily those of the Foundation. This exercise was commissioned by the project team: Margaret Flynn, Tricia Sloper, Lesley Hayes and Lesley Cotterill. My thanks to Lesley Hayes, Lesley Cotterill and Margaret Flynn, who established so much of the costs data and to the co-ordinators, managers and finance officers of the schemes who dealt so patiently with my follow-up queries. My thanks to Ken Wright and Kirsteen Smith for background material and to Tricia Sloper and Lesley Hayes for their comments on an earlier draft of this chapter.

Gerard, K. (1990) 'Economic evaluation of respite care for children with mental handicaps: a preliminary analysis of problems.' *Mental Handicap 18*, December.

Hayes, L., Flynn, M., Cotterill, L. and Sloper, T. (1995) *Respite Services for Adult Citizens with Learning Disabilities*. Report to The Joseph Rowntree Foundation. Manchester: National Development Team.

Knapp, M.R.J. (1993) 'Principles of applied cost research.' In A. Netten and J. Beecham (eds) *Costing Community Care: Theory and Practice*. Aldershot: Ashgate.

Knapp, M.R.J. (1995) *The Economic Evaluation of Mental Health Services*. Aldershot: Ashgate.

Levin, E., Moriarty, J. and Gorbach, P. (1994) *Better for the Break*. London: HMSO.

Netten, A. (1994a) *The Unit Costs of Community Care*. Personal Social Services Research Unit, University of Kent, Canterbury.

Netten, A. (1994b) *Costing Innovative Services for People with Learning Difficulties*. Personal Social Services Research Unit Discussion Paper 1100, University of Kent, Canterbury.

Netten, A. and Beecham, J. (eds) (1993) *Costing Community Care: Theory and Practice*. Aldershot: Ashgate.

Orlik, C., Robinson, C. and Russell, O. (1991) *A Survey of Family Based Respite Care Schemes in the United Kingdom*. Norah Fry Research Centre, University of Bristol.

Robinson, C. (1986) *Avon Short Term Respite Care Scheme Evaluation Study – Final Report: Part 2 – A More Detailed Look at the Results*. Department of Mental Health, University of Bristol.

Chapter 5

The Conundrum of Quality

Meg Lindsay

Introduction

The trouble with much discussion of quality in relation to 'respite' care services is that often there is no underlying agreement on what the service is there for in the first place. The result is that inappropriate quality indicators are chosen and the whole field becomes very confused.

In order to avoid this, it is essential to ask three questions at the outset – first, what is the *purpose* of any sort of 'respite' care service? Second, what *method* does the specific service under consideration use to fulfil that purpose? Third, what are the *indicators* which will show whether that particular service is good, bad or indifferent?

Terminology

In discussing these issues, the term 'respite' care will be used, even though the author is well aware and convinced of the pejorative nature of the term. My reason for using it is that all other terms seem to imply that a specific type of service will be delivered – 'short breaks' implying parting the carer and person cared for (and being only a little less pejorative in the process); 'home support' implying domiciliary care and so on. There is a need to look a little more closely at all the services that people are wont to call 'respite' in order to identify the common elements which lead to use of the term. This is not to suggest that individual services should be called 'respite' in their titles, as so often happens – the names of individual services should relate to the specific things they are actually doing, or better still, just where they happen to be situated.

In analysing some of the thinking behind this type of service, it is useful to look at how this term is used. As one does so, it becomes clear that there is some kind of shared understanding between professionals about the common element in these types of provision. This common element has to be highlighted, because the reason the term 'respite' has proved so hard to shift is that its core meaning has never been brought to the fore in a way that would enable another word to be found to describe the services so offered.

As has been said, most service providers have what might be called a 'subliminal' understanding of the purpose of 'respite' care, but lack the ability to put this into words. The underlying feeling seems to be that, whether services are provided at home or away from home, whether they are for a couple of hours a week, or four weeks at a time, the essence of the services – the factor that makes them 'respite' – relates to the balance of the relationship between the carer and the person cared for. In this sense they are unlike other services, which can be seen as focusing primarily on the needs of one person, or a group of people who can be seen to have the same needs. In the case of services that people identify as 'respite' care, there is a sense that there are differing needs interlinked by the relationship between those who have them. This appears to be confirmed by the fact that new types of services which attempt, through the intervention of alternative care arrangements, to protect relationships seen as being under stress, are also being called 'respite'. For example, this term is now regularly used to describe short-term removals from home of teenagers in cases where the stress between them and their parents has become acute. Here, the objective of the removal is to protect the relationship so as to avoid the need for long-term care.

Of course, there are other types of services offering 'short breaks', which are also described as 'respite'. Older people who live on their own may be offered a short stay with a family, in order to give them company, a chance to enjoy stimulating activities, and a break from the pressure of catering for themselves when this may be proving too onerous. Likewise, people who have a disability, or those who have mental health problems, may require and receive assistance to take a holiday. However, *this chapter focuses on services which have historically been called 'respite' and which involve both the carer and the person for whom they provide care.*

The purpose of 'respite' care

What then is the core purpose at the heart of the services called 'respite' care? As indicated above, the crucial issue appears to be the balance of the relationship between the carer and the person cared for. In short, *'respite' services are intended to assist two different types of service user simultaneously. These are, first, carers and, second, the people whom they care for. It is this interlinking between the two, and a recognition of their need for external assistance in maintaining a quality of life within their two roles, that is the definitive aspect of any 'respite' care service.*

When looked at in this light, it becomes clear that this balance is very difficult to achieve, and has often been overlooked in the past. It has been easy to see the purpose of 'respite' as being to 'give the carers a break', all the emphasis going on the needs of the carers for rest from the 'burden' of caring. More recently, and partly as a reaction to this focus on the needs of the carer, emphasis has been laid on the needs of the person requiring care to have opportunities to enjoy other experiences and relationships than those their carer can provide. The debates between these two approaches can be as forthright as they are unhelpful. In fact, such debates are really driven by professional agendas rather than those of service users. Carers, for example, often make it clear that they do not feel able to enjoy the supposed benefits to them of 'respite', when they are aware that the person they care for does not gain a corresponding benefit from the arrangement. Indeed, they can feel so guilty and vulnerable at having their supposed weakness and need for support thus heralded, that they may be unable to bring themselves to accept the offer of any service that is made. Likewise, the person receiving the care also has a voice and a view. In recent years, people who have disabilities have rightly become far more vocal about this issue, and it is essential that their opinion of the place of any so-called 'respite' service in their lives and priorities is clearly heard and taken into account. It is a vital dimension in the planning of any service which aims to meet their needs and those of their carers.

Method of fulfilling the purpose

If the overall objective of many types of 'respite' care is an attempt to preserve the quality of the lifestyle of the carer and the person cared for, then this means that at times they will require assistance to spend 'good quality' time apart as well as together. One way of approaching the issue of how to offer this appropriately is to consider how families who do not have a dependant member are able to organise their lifestyles. This comparison shows up clearly those areas in which access to the same opportunities is restricted for families with a disabled or frail member. If these 'gaps' can be 'plugged' then the family – including carer and person cared for – has a much better chance of enjoying the same type of lifestyle as other people in the population.

Spending time apart may involve 'respite' care away from home or at home. Either option may include the objective of providing planned opportunities for the carer and the person cared for to enjoy different activities with different social groups. In any family, members often spend time apart on a regular basis, perhaps through social activities which involve one partner and not the other, or visits to friends or relatives which involve children but not parents, or vice versa. If one of the family requires additional assistance and care, this kind of time apart may be provided through 'respite' care, and this is often described as *'planned respite'*.

Family groupings tend to take holidays in different combinations depending upon the age and stage of their members and their relationships one with the other. Where one member requires extra support, it may well be that the holidays will be planned differently. It is to meet this need that breaks of perhaps 7–14 days annually may be offered to that person, and this is often known as *'holiday respite'*.

In addition to this, time apart may be required in any family as a result of emergencies. This need is particularly difficult to meet where one member is frail or disabled, and indeed the provision of care in emergencies is often cited by carers as a circumstance causing particular anxiety. 'Respite' care therefore may have the objective of providing support on an emergency basis – *'emergency respite care'*.

Assisting someone else in the family with a whole range of personal tasks is not a demand made on families without a disabled or frail member. Excluding babyhood and occasional short illness, most individuals attend to their own self-care needs. Likewise, as children mature, they increasingly carry responsibility for their own actions and safety, and thereafter family members do not usually undertake these basic tasks for each other. Extra assistance is therefore required by families who have a member who may not be able to do these things for themselves, or cannot be left alone even for short periods while other members of the family go out and about. Day-to-day support at home of this nature is provided by *'domiciliary respite care'*.

There are other objectives which are met in general by both 'away from home' and home-based 'respite' care. The underlying purpose of much 'respite' care is the preservation of relationships within the family, so all members can enjoy a quality of life which other families may take for granted. This involves help in preserving family roles, economic security and the health and well-being of the carer. There is a considerable body of evidence showing that all these factors are affected detrimentally by the need to care (for example, Parker 1990, Twigg and Atkin 1991). The provision of support services which share responsibility for caring both at home and away from home are seen as central to preserving the carer's well-being and also resolving some of the inevitable stresses in a relationship between a carer and the person cared for.

It is important to recognise that the above methods of providing 'respite' care – planned, holiday, emergency and domiciliary – are all different ways of meeting the common purpose of 'respite' care services, which is to support the quality of life of the carer and person cared for. Therefore the core quality measure is how well each service does that, in keeping with its own approach.

For example, it is obviously important that a good planned 'respite' service will disrupt the day-to-day life of the person who is cared for as little as possible, and will enable them to keep quite closely to their usual routine. Further, it should be near to or even within their home that the support is offered, in familiar surroundings. On the other hand, holidays are necessarily a change from the normal daily routine of the holiday-maker, and they usually involve travelling a distance and living in unfamiliar surroundings. Therefore, what indicates a good model of holiday 'respite' will not necessarily indicate a good model of planned 'respite'.

This may seem obvious, but it is surprising how hard it seems to be to impress this idea on agencies at the time when new services are being designed. In one case known to the author, a service provider with premises in a particularly verdant rural area of the country discussed providing a good holiday 'respite' service. He was told by the local authority concerned that this would not be acceptable, as 'respite services should be locally based'. Planned services should be locally based, yes, but the general public is not crying out to their travel agents for holiday venues which are within one or two miles of their home.

Another problem caused by this lack of clarity about overall purpose and approach is the mixing of different methods within the one service. Thus one finds services which are combining emergency 'respite' care along with planned 'respite' care. The result is that people, who may well be distressed and confused, suddenly arrive in a setting where the staff are attempting to provide a calm and organised service for the other residents. The resident there as a result of an emergency may find that his/her needs do not receive appropriate attention, while the others risk having the stay that they have planned for and looked forward to, disrupted. Meanwhile, the carers of both are left uncertain as to what their relative will experience during any visit. There is also an ever-present danger of the cancellation of a planned stay at short notice, because of an emergency admission.

In terms of services designed to provide 'respite' support, emergency provision is usually the least well thought out. Ideally, the best way of supporting the relationship at such times is through a team approach from a number of service providers – domiciliary, residential, family based and others – who can look at the actual support needs of those concerned, and with them plan a composite response, which will also allow counselling and, if necessary, long-term planning to go alongside provision to meet immediate needs.

Summary

The crucial factor in choosing a method of providing support to a carer and person who is cared for is that it should be the best that it can be *of its type*. There is no point in applying general rules about the quality indicators which relate to a service, without considering very carefully what the 'blueprint' originally was – in other words, did the provider set out to meet the purpose of 'respite' by providing holidays, planned support, emergency back up or domiciliary care? To try to adopt general rules which apply to all, without recognising the essential differences, is akin to saying that a poodle with curly hair is a good example of a dog, and that therefore alsations are not good dogs because they have straight hair.

Indicators of quality in 'respite' care

Having noted that to produce quality services, providers must understand the basic purpose of 'respite' care, and must be clear in their minds about the method by which they intend to fulfil that purpose, it is now possible to look at quality indicators for any service claiming to provide this type of 'respite' care.

Time and again, throughout the literature, in conversations with carers, with their relatives and with professionals, the same range of qualities is picked out as being indicative of 'good quality' 'respite' care. These are: *flexibility, accessibility, and involvement of the carer and the person requiring care in the design and delivery of the service* (Lindsay et al. 1993).

Flexibility

One of the aspects that is looked for in a total package of care offered to the family with a frail or disabled member is flexibility. It need not necessarily be evident in each individual facet of support services, but the total effect of the package of care must be to respond meaningfully, at short notice, to the everyday changes and fluctuations in the rhythm of life.

A common fear among carers is that some emergency will overtake them and there will be no service flexible enough to be able to adapt itself to the altered situation. Further, inflexibility of the services surrounding them can affect the whole lifestyle of the carer, and with it that of their relative. Carers are less likely to be in employment than their peers who are not carers, and more likely to suffer economic loss as a result of their caring role (Twigg and Atkin 1991, Geall 1991). If services were less dictated by the needs of the service provider, and more by the needs of the carer, it would be easier for the latter to take up or to maintain employment. For example, the early closing times of day centres mean that it is very difficult for carers to consider any work that is not very part-time in nature. Some domiciliary services also work 9 to 5, meaning that assistance with getting someone out of bed and ready for day-centre transport falls solely to the carer, with much the same effect.

Flexibility can be difficult for services to build in, creating logistical problems. It requires imagination and determination to overcome these, through liaison with other service providers and creative use of existing staff. The fact that such aspects of the service are rarely built in at the design stage, and seldom allowed for later, indicates that service providers are not really aware that this is a key quality indicator as far as families are concerned.

Accessibility

Accessibility to services involves a range of factors. It relates to the ability of the carer and user to find out that the service exists in the first place, and to travel to and from it. It also involves the cost they may have to pay or expenses they may incur by using it, the application procedure, and cultural, social class or related factors which may make the service unacceptable. Each of these is discussed briefly below.

INFORMATION

As one carer put it, 'It's hard to ask for something when you do not know that it exists' (Lindsay *et al.* 1993). A recurring theme in talking to carers, echoed in the literature, is that they do not use services because they do not know the services are there (Robinson and Stalker 1991). It is a common experience in many agencies that referrals are received from people who have been in need of the service for some time, but simply did not know of its existence and so could not make use of it.

Similarly, new services often report low uptake until they become known. Ease of access to information therefore must be seen as a clear indicator of the quality of any service.

DISTANCE AND TRAVEL

Services may be developed which are highly effective and offer expert care but which necessitate long journeys for the individual using them. This is a particular problem in rural areas, where population density is lower. Even if the carer is not involved in providing the transport, the journeys travelled by people who have discomfort in sitting, or who may be restless, can be extremely lengthy. Even when the 'respite' care service may be fairly local to the individual's day centre or home, 'pick up' routes may mean that someone is sitting in a bus for an hour and a half, or even two hours, in order to reach the service.

It is also not uncommon for services to be established without a budget for the fairly substantial transport costs which can be involved. This again results in the carer providing transport, often at awkward times, and thus for them a poor experience of service quality.

COST

Many studies have shown clearly the damaging effect on the overall income of the family of the special care needs of one member (for example, Carers' National Association 1992). Because many carers are on restricted incomes, services which charge may be less accessible to a large number of potential users than one would wish. The amount someone has to pay for a service markedly affects its accessibility and, thus, its usefulness. The way this issue is handled has a direct effect on the quality of service users' experience.

APPLICATION PROCEDURE

The procedure which a carer and potential user have to go through in order to access a service may greatly affect their freedom to use it. There is no doubt that lengthy procedures involving assessment and selection panels, and the unilateral offering of 'slots of care' at the convenience of the service provider, can result in dissatisfaction for the carers. They may feel that the service is offered at times which are inconvenient to them or which do not allow them to plan other activities which they would like to pursue when their relative is either absent or being cared for by someone else in their own home.

The balance between allocating services fairly and on a basis of assessed need while, on the other hand, ensuring that service providers work in partnership with carers and those cared for is a difficult one, but is key to the accessibility and therefore the quality of service provision.

CULTURAL, ETHNIC AND SOCIAL CLASS FACTORS

There is an increasing body of literature regarding the acceptability and suitability of 'respite' services to people from ethnic minority groups. Research has shown (Lenehan 1981, Baxter et al. 1990, McCalman 1990) that to date they are substantially less happy with services offered to them than people from the majority community, and also make disproportionately less use of them.

It is particularly important that carers should feel that their religious and cultural identities will be maintained, both by alternative carers coming into the home for domiciliary support purposes and also by residential or family-based services to which their relative may go. This is equally true of particular religious differences within mainstream culture.

In the case of social class, evidence is increasingly coming to light that people in socio-occupational classes 4 and 5 are less likely to uptake 'respite' care services than those from social classes 1, 2 and 3 (Robinson and Stalker 1991). The exact reasons for this are not yet clear. However, a service cannot claim to be of high quality when users or potential users feel uncomfortable and alienated by the style in which it is offered.

Partnership with user and carer

In many ways, this is the real key to quality in 'respite' care services. If the concept of partnership is genuinely taken on board and the service is built around it, then much of what has been described above will happen as a matter of course.

The significant and very real difference that sets 'respite' services apart is, as has been described, that they are designed simultaneously to meet the needs of two sets of people – the carer and the cared-for person. In most other situations, the service provider also becomes the *main carer*. Older people in nursing homes, children in residential settings, patients in hospitals, all relate directly to those providing the care, and negotiation about how that care should be delivered is carried out between them. In the case of 'respite' care, the *main carer* is *not* the service provider, despite the fact that the person cared for is resident within the service or is regularly receiving attention from it. The main carer is still the husband, wife, daughter, son and so on. Understanding this is the key to appreciating why there can be so much discontent with 'respite' services on the part of the carer. Often, the cared-for person returns home wearing inappropriate clothing; little ailments they may have had while away have not been reported to the carer; tiny details about the person which the carer wishes to give have not been asked for or noted down. The domiciliary service may not adapt to household practices subtly, but may imply or even suggest that they 'know a better way'. The service providers can appear to, or actually do, overrule the carer's normal patterns and routines of care, thus upsetting the rhythm of life for carer and user alike.

The skill and priority of a good 'respite' care service provider is to match the care offered seamlessly into the way of life of the people concerned. 'Respite' care need not be a replica of that life – the experience of 'respite' care has to match that life, and enhance it. What it must not do is clash with it, and create disharmony.

In any service, there are norms and cultures, sometimes formalised as policy and procedure, sometimes taking the form of custom and practice. When people utilise a service for the minority of their time, they bring with them a great variety of norms and cultures, and if the priority is to 'match seamlessly' with their way of life at home, then the service has to develop a chameleon-like ability to change its practices and norms according to the people currently using it, while still adhering to basic underlying principles of good care practice. This applies equally to services of all types – residential, family-based, hospital, domiciliary.

Much weight has been given to the need for partnership between carers and professionals (Pitkeathley 1989), but there is no doubt that the balance of power still rests very much with the professional who holds the budget. Whoever controls the services and 'gatekeeps' on the use of them has the real power.

More attempts are now being made to involve carers and users in service delivery, however. Current thinking about quality has encouraged this by defining quality services from the point of view of the consumer. However, it must not be forgotten that many carers find it difficult to use 'respite' care services because they feel firmly that the person who needs the care is their responsibility first and foremost. If agencies do not demonstrate that they recognise the primacy of the views of the person cared for and the carer in the design and delivery of their services, then by this attitude they create a hurdle for potential users which many will not feel able to surmount.

Conclusion

How then do we begin to understand what quality 'respite' services of this type should look like? What are the essential things which must be present, and if absent, then however good everything else may be, the service cannot be described as 'top notch'?

These 'touchstones' centre around how well any service sets out to support both the carer and the person they care for, so that they can have a balanced and 'normal' lifestyle, and so that their relationship can continue undamaged by the demands placed upon it. This support can come in a variety of forms, venues and styles, but it must be flexible, accessible, and represent a genuine and meaningful partnership.

References

Baxter, C., Poonia, K., Ward, L. and Nadirshaw, Z. (1990) *Double Discrimination: Issues and Services for People with Learning Disabilities from Black and Ethnic Minority Communities*. London: King's Fund Centre/Commission for Racial Equality.

Carers' National Association (1992) *London. Speak Up, Speak Out*. London: Carers' National Association.

Geall, R. (1991) *Sharing the Caring – Respite Care for Children and Families*. London: National Children's Homes.

Lenehan, C. (1981) *Respite Care in the East End: A Multi-cultural Challenge*. London: Barnardos.

Lindsay, M., Kohls, J. and Collins, J. (1993) *The Patchwork Quilt – A Study of Respite Care Services in Scotland*. Edinburgh: The Scottish Office.

McCalman, J.A. (1990) *The Forgotten Community – Carers in Three Minority Ethnic Communities in Southwark*. London: King's Fund Centre and Help the Aged, SCEMSC.

Parker, G. (1990) *With Due Care and Attention – A Review of the Research on Informal Care*. London: Family Policy Studies Centre.

Pitkeathley, J. (1989) *It's My Duty, Isn't It?* London: Souvenir Press.

Robinson, C. and Stalker, K. (1991) *Respite Care – Summaries and Suggestions. The Final Report to the Department of Health*. Norah Fry Research Centre, University of Bristol.

Twigg, J. and Atkin, K. (1991) *Evaluating Support to Informal Carers – Summary Report*. University of York.

Chapter 6

Breaks for Disabled Children

Carol Robinson

There are currently 360,000 disabled children in Britain under the age of 16, 98 per cent of whom live at home with their families (OPCS 1989). The stress associated with caring for a disabled child has been well documented (Wilkin 1979, Glendinning 1983, Pahl and Quine 1984, Buckle 1984, Baldwin 1985). More recently, the NCH Action for Children (1994) and Beresford (1994) have examined the experiences of disabled children and their families and, in so doing, have highlighted the love and commitment parents show towards their children. At the same time, Beresford, like others before (OPCS 1989, Bose 1991, Baldwin and Carlisle 1994), emphasises the importance of short-term breaks as a source of support to parents.

The development of short-term breaks has already been covered in Chapter 1. This chapter will therefore begin with an examination of the research evidence on the range and availability of services, followed by a summary of parents' and children's views of those services. The remainder of the chapter will be devoted to identifying new ways of creating breaks for children which also provide positive experiences for them.

The range and availability of short-term breaks

According to the most recent figures available from Shared Care UK, in 1992 there were 257 family-link services for children in operation in Britain, catering for approximately 10,000 children (Beckford and Robinson 1993). Comparable data are not available for the numbers using residential homes for short-term care, although an estimated 7800 beds were found to be available in Britain in 1991 (Geall 1991). Some of these were in local authority homes, others in health authority group homes and special units.

There is no reliable information available on the numbers of children who are hospitalised to give their parents a break. However, research by Robinson and Stalker (1989) revealed that in three local authority areas, within a 12-month period, 31 children had episodes of short-term care in hospital wards or health authority units. In a further three cases, children had prolonged stays in actual wards, in one case lasting three years. This probably represents an underestimate of the total numbers because many more hospital records stated 'pseudo-medical' reasons for admissions, suggesting a desire to provide 'respite' for parents lay behind the decision to admit the child.

Hospices also offer short-term care to children with life-threatening conditions, although there is no research documenting the numbers of families who receive support from them. One hospice alone has supported 260 families via short-term care placements (Martin House, personal communication 1994).

Family-based short-term care is substantially over-subscribed, according to two national surveys conducted by Shared Care UK. In 1992, 91 per cent of family-link services had a waiting list, with average numbers waiting having increased from 14 to 18 per scheme between 1990 and 1992 (Beckford and Robinson 1993). Similarly, 82 per cent of befriending schemes, which enable children to have one-to-one support from a volunteer companion, had a waiting list. Waiting lists for residential short-term care appear to be rare, although popular units may simply reduce the average number of days of care available in order to accommodate everyone 'on their books' (Robinson and Stalker 1990).

Who uses services and why?

According to Geall (1991), only 5 per cent of disabled children use any form of short-term care, although the figure is likely to be higher amongst the most severely disabled group (17% according to the OPCS survey 1989).

The indications from research are that the type of service used by families is not random. For example, children from minority ethnic groups are much more likely to use health service facilities than either family-link schemes or local authority-run establishments (Robinson and Stalker 1989). Similarly, certain groups are much less likely to have a family link than others. These include young people who have challenging behaviours, children over the age of ten years, those who are profoundly disabled and require lifting, as well as children from low-income families and pupils of residential schools.

There are a variety of reasons why each of these groups may find family-link services inaccessible or unattractive. First, not all families have access to the relevant information either because it is not sufficiently widely publicised or because it is not presented in a format that they can understand. Indeed, in Sloper and Turner's 1992 study, 59 per cent of parents said that their greatest need was for more information. According to parents in one study, a lack of information about one family-link service accounted for 16 per cent of non-use (Robinson 1986).

Second, service providers in many areas face a general lack of family-link carers and experience problems placing some children who have challenging behaviour or high levels of need (Orlik, Robinson and Russell 1990, Stalker and Robinson 1991).

Third, there is evidence that family-link carers are predominantly white and middle class (Robinson 1986, Stalker 1991, Beckford and Robinson 1993). This may mean that families who are on low incomes and from minority ethnic groups are less likely to be attracted to such schemes. Equally, if they do apply, they may find themselves offered inappropriate links or waiting for long periods until a suitable family is found (Shah 1992).

One final plausible explanation is that some parents offered a family link may have difficulty using the system to their benefit, since many services still try to retain a very informal approach which involves parents asking for breaks when they need them. Clearly this places at a disadvantage those who are least confident and articulate.

Multiple users

In contrast to families who have poor access to services, there is a significant minority of families (between 18 and 21% depending on the area) who use several services (Robinson and Stalker 1989). These families are unable to get adequate support from one service and therefore use two or more during the year. The group of children most likely to be affected are those who require high levels of supervision or care. Concern arises, therefore, about the impact that moving from one care setting to another may have on the child's behaviour. In the worst cases, this may create a downward spiral in his or her behaviour, which leads to the parents deciding to place the child in long-term care (Oswin 1984).

Trickett and Lee (1989) highlight similar problems associated with children attending residential schools who require short-term care in school holidays. They point to the lack of safeguards available for such children and question the appropriateness of multiple placements which lead to children spending very little time at home.

Unfortunately, despite the Children Act 1989, which came into force in 1991, there remain no appropriate legal safeguards for children whose short-term care exceeds the recommended ceiling of 90 days. With the emergence of a series of papers on short-term care by the Department of Health between August 1994 and August 1995, there was the potential to remove this loophole in the existing regulations, at least for children in England and Wales. Unfortunately this opportunity has not been seized and the Children (short-Term Placements) 'Miscellaneous Amendments' Regulations 1995, increased the ceiling from 90 days' to 120 days' care. This amendment has served only to legitimise extensive periods away from home without clear guidance on how to protect children who are in this position. Happily, other amendments in these regulations are likely to strengthen good practice whilst reducing some of the burden of bureaucracy of which many social workers complained.

Parents' views of services

Beresford (1994) highlights the suspicion felt by some parents of young disabled children towards short-term breaks. Anxiety about the effect on the child, coupled with a belief that parental responsibility should not be shared, has similarly been documented by Stalker (1991) and Robinson (1986). These parents appear to constitute about 15 per cent of those eligible to use short-break services (Robinson and Stalker 1992). For this group, the traditional model of 'away from home' care is unlikely to offer an acceptable form of support (Cohen and Warren 1985). However, changing the pattern of service delivery to include more domiciliary arrangements might increase uptake. This is supported by findings from the OPCS survey (1989), which indicate that 23 per cent of parents of disabled children aged 0–4 years want domiciliary services, while 52 per cent of parents in another study said they wanted to keep their children at home (Robinson 1987).

Undoubtedly, some parents may be forced to use services which are not satisfactory if there is no other option available to them (Hubert 1991). However, most parents express satisfaction with the short-term care they use. In a national study of consumer views of all services on offer, family-based care (family-link) was found to be the source of greatest satisfaction (Robinson and Stalker 1990). Although some parents of severely disabled children who needed nursing care were more satisfied with health authority units than with residential homes run by local authorities, there was very little difference in the overall levels of satisfaction expressed by the two. However, there were some concerns in both groups about poor *physical* care and these concerns constituted about one-third of all those expressed by each group.

Poor physical care, including over-dosing of residents to make them more manageable, was also documented by Hubert (1991), who gives a very worrying account of the poor care received by a group of profoundly disabled young people in two health authority establishments. However, there is nothing to indicate that such inadequate care is widespread. In the national study mentioned above, other issues were raised by parents in connection with both types of residential facility. These related to the behaviour of other children, the lack of personal care, the loss of the child's usual routine and inadequate safety measures (Robinson and Stalker 1990). In contrast, high levels of satisfaction have been found where there is emphasis on high standards of child care, flexibility around arrangements for stays and plenty of parental involvement (Brimblecombe and Russell 1987).

Many parents also experience problems in obtaining breaks when they want them (Stalker and Robinson 1991), especially where residential homes operate an advance booking system or have large numbers of users. However, as already indicated, some control over the frequency of the stays away from home is likely to be in the best interests of the child, especially if there is a risk of drift into long-term care (Russell 1995).

In addition to short-term care, families often need different support services which help them to address other problems they may encounter. Beresford (1994) pointed out that in some of the families she interviewed, the disabled child was not necessarily the main source of stress and parents expressed needs for a wide variety of services from professionals. Help with benefits and financial management was one such service she identified and this has been confirmed by the NCH Action for Children (1994). Similarly, practical assistance which relieves the difficulties associated with day-to-day care of the child, as well as help with family relationships, may both be required at various times (Russell 1995).

Other ways of getting a break

Given the relatively low numbers of disabled children using short-term care services and the concern expressed by some families about the traditional models of service delivery, there is a need to consider alternative ways of creating breaks. Increasingly, services are aiming to provide a positive experience for the children they serve as well as giving parents a break from their caring role. However, there remain some services which do little to enhance social opportunities or personal development. This section will try to give a flavour of some of the most interesting initiatives in creating breaks, drawing on examples from the UK, Scandinavia, Australia and the US.

Brief reference has already been made to befriending services. These schemes offer an opportunity to teenagers and adults to go out with a friend on a regular basis and become involved in activities that interest both parties. Such services exist in many parts of the UK and Australia. Perhaps partly because they rely heavily on volunteers who are paid expenses and/or a small allowance, they appear to experience some difficulties maintaining befriending arrangements on a long-term basis. None the less, these services offer great scope for tailoring joint activities to the individual's personal preferences and generally provide a more natural break than pre-planned stays away from home.

Two services in the UK, which started life as residential short-term care units, developed along similar lines. Both have invested time and energy into setting up a wide range of recreational opportunities for children. These include a range of evening and weekend activities which incorporate horse-riding, dry-slope skiing, water sports, drama and craft workshops. In addition, one of the services has developed a small network of family links and young befrienders. Other options include taking children away for weekends and holidays, as well as staff accompanying families on holiday to share the care and supervision of the young person.

However, a growing recognition that holidays away from home did little to help integrate the children into their local community led to a shift in emphasis, with staff supporting children in attending local groups such as brownies, youth clubs and evening classes. Ultimately, the aim of such an exercise was to give the young person sufficient confidence to attend alone. The overall impact of these community-based initiatives has been a dramatic reduction in the need for residential beds. One of these homes has now closed completely and the other only requires two beds to be available.

In America, co-operative sitting arrangements have developed in which families with disabled children care for other disabled children on a reciprocal basis (Salisbury and Intagliata 1986). They do not have to pay for the service, although a co-ordinator recruits families into the co-operative and arranges the sessions on their behalf. Whilst this kind of service does not guarantee a positive experience for the child, it does ensure that the young person is not moved out of his/her usual environment and yet is likely to be familiar with the sitter. With minor modifications this type of arrangement could be improved: sitters could be given training relating to the needs of individual children and an assurance required that no new sitters would provide care until they have met all the children involved. Moreover, the service would become more attractive for the children if the sitter's children became friends with whom they could spend time.

In Sweden, there is a legal entitlement to short-term care (Ministry of Health and Social Affairs 1986). Here, the concept of summer camps is well understood and such facilities are widely used by families of disabled and non-disabled children alike. Parents must pay for these, since they are seen as providing a summer holiday in the countryside. A wide range of outdoor activities is generally on offer and the emphasis is on 'having fun'. Summer camps run for up to three weeks a year and children tend to go back to the same holiday site year after year. In this way, camp leaders are likely to be familiar to the children after their first stay. Many disabled children go to special rather than integrated camps, although integrated facilities are becoming increasingly available (Robinson 1989).

Potentially, summer camps offer a very positive experience to children, but inadequate preparation and unfamiliar personal carers could jeopardise this. To be a really valuable resource, it is likely that parents would need to be involved in visiting the camp site with the child, being properly briefed about the activities on offer and agreeing what level of risk they are prepared for their child to undertake. Moreover, any personal carers would need to get to know the child and his/her preferences prior to the holiday. Finally, offering friends and siblings opportunities to accompany the child could both increase the latter's enjoyment and provide some safeguards against potential abuse.

A number of integrated after-school services have been developed by 'Playworks' in Victoria, Australia. This agency offers disabled children opportunities to participate in local child-care services before and after school and in school holidays. In so doing, it provides support and promotes inclusion in existing services, thus allowing parents who wish to take paid work the opportunity to do so (George 1992).

Another initiative which also holds the potential to provide parents with the chance to take up employment is the training of 'special' child-minders. South Glamorgan County Council in Wales is currently considering this idea (Spence 1994) and Salford City Council sponsors child-minders already. Ideally, if children are to benefit fully, these child-minders should take a mix of disabled and non-disabled children rather than only disabled children. Although there is a risk that a small pool of trained people will soon become over-committed, this idea seems to offer real choices to parents of children under eight who have hitherto been unable to contemplate paid work (Baldwin 1985).

The above list of service developments is not by any means comprehensive, although many of the most interesting projects are based on similar themes, namely integration and normalisation. Despite these exciting possibilities, most short-term care services remain unimaginative and limited by resources. In the worst cases, they are harmful to the direct users (Hubert 1991). The developments described above often involve one-to-one care and it is vital that appropriate checks and safeguards are incorporated into new services if disabled children are not to be made even more vulnerable than they already are (Conroy, Fielding and Tunstill 1990).

Sadly there is little evidence on the cost effectiveness of these innovative schemes, although per capita costs of family-based care and residential facilities demonstrate the economic argument for the former type of provision (Gerard 1990). In her chapter in this volume, Netten looks at costs in relation to an innovative approach to providing breaks for adults with learning difficulties. There is a pressing need to evaluate the cost effectiveness of some of the newest children's services, if policy-makers are to take up the challenge of creating more child-centred and integrated options.

Conclusions

Short-term breaks for disabled children have undoubtedly changed considerably in the last decade, not only in the UK but also in the US, Canada, Australia, New Zealand and Scandinavia. However, a similar rate of change is not apparent in continental Europe where residential provision is widespread, and family-based schemes poorly developed (Watchel 1994, Zelderloo 1994,[1] personal communications with the author).

At present, many services which could offer support to families fail to do so because they do not adequately publicise their availability. Others fail to take account of the different social and cultural backgrounds of potential users and thereby exclude some of the families who most need them. Undoubtedly, one of the greatest challenges is to develop ways of providing regular and enjoyable breaks for children with challenging behaviour and complex or profound disabilities. Effort must go into developing individual plans for these children which are both financially and emotionally sustainable. This means extensive planning and adequate training for short-term carers, coupled with the establishment of on-going and emergency support systems (Robinson and Stalker 1992).

To succeed, community care must be based on imaginative ideas, backed up by adequate resources. Without this, many of the children who are currently 'most difficult to accommodate' in short-term services may find themselves in long-term care.

References

Baldwin, S.M. (1985) *The Costs of Caring: Families with Disabled Children.* London: Routledge and Kegan Paul.

Baldwin, S. and Carlisle, J. (1994) *Social Support for Disabled Children and their Families. A Review of the Literature.* Social Work Services Inspectorate, Edinburgh. HMSO.

---

1   A researcher at the University of Oldenberg, Germany, and Service co-ordinator, Begeleindinscentum Sint Franciscus, Belgium, respectively.

Beckford, V. and Robinson, C. (1993) *Consolidation or Change? A Second Survey of Family Based Respite Care Services in the UK.* Bristol: Shared Care UK.

Beresford, B. (1994) *Positively Parents. Caring for a Severely Disabled Child.* Social Policy Research Unit, University of York. London: HMSO.

Bose, R. (1991) 'The effect of a family support scheme on maternal mental health of mothers caring for children with mental handicaps.' *Research, Policy and Planning 9*, 1, 2–8.

Brimblecombe, F. and Russell, P. (1987) *Honeylands: Developing a Service for Families with Handicapped Children.* London: National Children's Bureau.

Buckle, J. (1984) 'The massive costs of raising a mentally handicapped child.' *DIB Around,* 13 March. Disability Income Group.

Cohen, S. and Warren, R. (1985) *Respite Care, Principles, Programs and Policies.* Austin, Texas: Pro-Ed Inc.

Conroy, S., Fielding, N.G. and Tunstill, J. (1990) *Investigating Child Sexual Abuse: The Study of a Joint Initiative.* London: London Police Federation.

Department of Health (1994) Consultation paper on short-term placements (respite care of children). Issued August, London.

Department of Health (1995) The Children Act (Short-Term Placements) (Miscellaneous Amendments Regulations). London: HMSO.

Geall, R. (1991) *Sharing the Caring. Respite Care in the UK for Families and Children with Disabilities.* Action for Children. London: National Children's Homes.

George, J. (1992) *Victorian Respite Services for Children with a Disability.* State Report to Third National Conference organised by Interchange Inc and held in Canberra, October.

Gerard, K. (1990) 'Economic evaluation of respite care for children with mental handicaps: a preliminary analysis of problems.' *Mental Handicap 18,* December, 150–155.

Glendinning, C. (1983) *Unshared Care: Parents and their Disabled Children.* London: Routledge and Kegan Paul.

Hubert, J. (1991) *Home-bound: Crisis in the Care of Young People with Severe Learning Difficulties.* London: King's Fund Centre.

Ministry of Health and Social Affairs, Sweden (1986) Special Services for Intellectually Handicapped Persons Act. International Secretariat, Stockholm, Sweden.

National Children's Homes Action for Children (1994) *Unequal Opportunities. Children with Disabilities and Their Families Speak Out.* London: NCH.

Office of Population Censuses and Surveys (1989) Meltzer, H., Smyth, M. and Robus, N. Report 6. *Disabled Children. Services, Transport and Education.* London: HMSO.

Orlik, C., Robinson, C. and Russell, O. (1990) *A Survey of Family Based Respite Care Schemes in the UK.* Shared Care UK, Norah Fry Research Centre, Bristol.

Oswin, M. (1984) *They Keep Going Away: A Critical Study of Short Term Residential Care Services for Children who are Mentally Handicapped.* London: King's Fund Centre.

Pahl, J. and Quine, L. (1984) *Families with Mentally Handicapped Children: A Study of Stress and of Service Response.* University of Kent, Health Services Research Unit.

Robinson, C. (1986) *Avon Short Term Respite Care Scheme – Evaluation Study Part II. A More Detailed Look at the Results.* Department of Mental Health, University of Bristol.

Robinson, C. (1987) *Taking a Break. A Study of Respite Care for Families Living in Bristol and Weston Health District.* Department of Mental Health, University of Bristol.

Robinson, C. (1989) 'Respite care Swedish style.' Unpublished paper. Norah Fry Research Centre, University of Bristol.

Robinson, C. and Stalker, K. (1989) *Time for a Break. Respite Care: A Study of Providers, Consumers and Patterns of Use.* First interim report to the Department of Health. Norah Fry Research Centre, University of Bristol.

Robinson, C. and Stalker, K. (1990) *Respite Care: The Consumer's View.* Second interim report to the Department of Health. Norah Fry Research Centre, University of Bristol.

Robinson, C. and Stalker, K. (1992) *Why are We Waiting? Reducing Waiting Lists – Practical Guidance for Developing Short Term Breaks.* London: HMSO.

Russell, P. (1995) *The Children Act 1989. Children and Young People with Learning Disabilities – Some Opportunities and Challenges.* London: National Development Team and National Children's Bureau.

Salisbury, C. and Intagliata, J. (eds) (1986) *Respite Care Support for Persons with Developmental Disabilities and their Families.* Baltimore: Paul H. Brookes.

Shah, R. (1992) *The Silent Minority. Children with Disabilities in Asian Families.* London: National Children's Bureau.

Sloper, P. and Turner, S. (1992) 'Service needs of families of children with severe physical disability.' *Child: Care, Health and Development 18,* 5, 259–282.

Spence, C. (1994) Untitled paper presented to Children with Disability Working Group, South Glamorgan County Council.

Stalker, K. (1991) *Share the Care: An Evaluation of a Family Based Respite Care Service.* London: Jessica Kingsley Publishers.

Stalker, K. and Robinson, C. (1991) *You're on the Waiting List.* Third Interim Report to the Department of Health, Families Waiting for Respite Care Services. Norah Fry Research Centre, University of Bristol.

Trickett, S. and Lee, F. (1989) 'Children first?' *Community Care,* 26 January, 15–17.

Wilkin, D. (1979) *Caring for the Mentally Handicapped Child.* London: Croom Helm.

Chapter 7

Family-based Short-Term Breaks for Children in Need

Marie Bradley and Jane Aldgate

Introduction

In *all* families, some times are harder than others. Some stages in the life cycle of the family are inherently stressful and, as a consequence, the integrity of the family and the well-being of its members may be more vulnerable to pressure and disruption (Ignatieff 1992). We know this from our own experiences in families, those we grew up in and those we create. The birth of a child, adolescence, transitions and changes in the family, illness, separations and losses are both pivotal and demanding. On the whole, we know that at times like these, we turn to our family and friends for practical help and emotional support to give us a breathing space – time for ourselves, time to take stock and time to revise our strategies, if necessary. A temporary rest or relief from daily responsibilities, respite from the everyday wear and tear of family life, allows us to recharge our batteries (Aldgate, Pratt and Duggan 1989).

For various reasons, some families cannot look to their relatives and friends for this support and must turn to services outside the family. In a study of short-term care services for children in need, carried out for the Department of Health, Jane Aldgate, Marie Bradley and David Hawley explored arrangements for short-term family-based breaks with 60 such families (Aldgate, Bradley and Hawley 1995). In the first year of the study the provision of existing short-term accommodation for children in need was reviewed, and an interesting and eclectic range of models was found. In the subsequent phase of the study, the work of several short-term care schemes was examined in detail (Bradley and Aldgate 1995).

Terminology and legislation

It is worth making some comments about the terminology used in this chapter. When the study began, all the schemes involved offered 'respite care', a term which was used by families and workers to mean a short break, usually for *both* child and parent. The emphasis is different – parents have a break from day-to-day caring and children have an alternative experience of family life – but the notion of the breaks as *temporary*, and as *supportive* of the family unit was central to the arrangements (Department of Health 1991a). Somehow, 'respite' now seems to lack the clarity which past use implied, and we are searching for a term which adequately and simply reflects the quality and purpose of 'respite' care, without its disadvantages (see Chapter 1 of this volume). We have decided on the use of 'short-term breaks' as a 'working' definition, since it describes what is offered, and gives a flavour of the co-operative nature of the work between family, carer and agency (Gibbons 1992).

'Short-term accommodation' describes the intervention literally and legally, though it carries rather formal and statutory connotations. This term is defined in Regulation 13 of the Children Act 1989 Guidance and Regulations as follows (Department of Health 1991b):

> '[It] allows for a series of short, pre-planned placements... with the same carer to be treated as a single placement. Typically, these placements may be for regular staying contact or to allow the carer or the child to have a break... The conditions that such a series of placements have to meet to be treated as a single placement... are:
>
> (a) all the placements occur within a period which does not ex-ceed one year;
>
> (b) no single placement is for a duration of more than four weeks; and
>
> (c) the total duration of the placement does not exceed 90 days.'

Part 3 of the Children Act draws together local authorities' principal functions in respect of children, which include the identification of children in need, and the support of children's links with their families. A child is 'in need' if:

> '(a) he is unlikely to achieve or maintain, or to have the opportu-nity of achieving or maintaining, a reasonable standard of health

or development without the provision for him of services by a local authority under this Part;

(b) his health or development is likely to be significantly impaired, or further impaired, without the provision for him of such services; or

(c) he is disabled.' (Children Act 1989, Part 3, Section 17(10))

The study considered children in the categories (a) and (b), though many of the findings hold for those in the third category as well. These are children for whom the possibility of optimum, or 'good enough', development is likely to be impaired if help is not available from outside the family. Development may suffer in the specific sense, for example, when a child is unable to make progress in school because of worry and stress at home, and in the general sense, when long-standing difficulties at home mean that his life chances are restricted. The needs of such children are often most cogently brought to mind by considering their family circumstances. Long-standing disadvantages – poverty, unemployment, social isolation, broken family networks and single parenthood – may render some families, at some times in their lives, very vulnerable (National Council of Voluntary Child Care Organisations (NCCVO) 1991, Ignatieff 1992).

The linchpin of the Children Act is the concept of 'the child in the family in the community' as the most favourable context for growth and development. Wherever possible, it endorses and enables parental responsibility, including the development and use of a range of voluntary arrangements which help to keep the child in the family (Department of Health 1991a). Short-term accommodation arrangements can be a vital part of maintaining that possibility for children and families during periods of stress and vulnerability, holding the family together in times of difficulty, conserving and building on its strengths in a way that makes it stronger for the future (Aldgate 1993). Both practice and research show that the welfare of the child is always best achieved within the family. The sense of rightfully belonging and the assumptions which this allows about oneself, are not and should not be easily replaced. Short-term accommodation is then, in several senses, a 'family affair'. It meets the needs of both parent and child, through creating a link with another family in the community. Parents want – and get – some breathing space, sometimes for specific purposes and sometimes 'just a break'. Children – at least those other than adolescents – do not often ask for a break, but do, in most instances, enjoy and benefit from them. The needs of children are, in a very real sense, met by supporting and enabling their parents to meet those needs in the most fundamental sense – reliable, good enough care.

In our culturally complex society, viable families come in many shapes and sizes. The role of all families is to provide for some, at times most, of the physical and emotional needs of its members, and to prepare them for their part in society. The extent to which the family can or should meet these needs depends on the resources of the family and on the stage in the family and individual life cycle at which the need arises. Form and style of family life in modern Britain is rich and diverse, and our provision of services must reflect and support that richness and diversity (NCCVO 1991).

Models of service provision

The models identified in practice seem to correspond to the diversity of needs in different families, at different stages. Before looking more closely at some significant aspects of provision, the range of services for children in need is considered in outline. While a comprehensive overview of the provision of short-term breaks in England and Wales has not yet been attempted, it seems that it is far from universal. Schemes are more frequently found in urban areas, and for children in need they seem to be most frequently, though not exclusively, provided by the local authorities. Specific models identified were as follows:

- Brief, intensive provision of family-based short-term accommodation, where arrangements are made during a *specific period* of difficulty, usually defined by the parent. Typically, this offered weekly breaks for approximately three months or so, and the breaks generally covered one or two nights away from home. Ongoing difficulties are recognised but intervention is often prompted by crisis.

- Longer term, less intensive provision of short-term care where family difficulties are recognised as ongoing and associated with social circumstances such as unemployment, isolation and poverty, and intervention is supportive of family coping and change.

- Family-based or residential short-term care for adolescents in the course of achieving interdependence between their families and the community.

- Residential short-term care for adolescents who are returning home, having been accommodated in either residential or foster care.

- Short-term breaks in support of long-term foster placements.

- Short-term care for the children of families affected by serious health problems.

The study looked at the first two of these services, that is brief, intensive provision of family-based short-term care during a specific period of difficulty, generally weekly breaks for a period of about three months, and, second, families having longer term, less intensive provision where family difficulties are identified as ongoing, and are associated with social circumstances such as unemployment, isolation and poverty.

Short-term care arrangements were made as a single supportive intervention, or as part of a package of interventions. In the latter case, some elements of the 'package' address specific difficulties, while others are supportive of the family and help to facilitate change. In general, short-term arrangements seem to offer most when they are part of a co-ordinated plan to give breathing space and to undertake work which uses and builds on family strengths to provide long-term, effective strategies for the future.

Parents' views of short-term breaks
In this section, some of the views and experiences of the families we talked to are recorded. The arrangements were made with schemes which cover both county and city areas. Although each family and each arrangement is highly individual in its own way, they share common features. Many of the families were headed by a single parent, generally the mother. Parents were not especially young, most were between 25 and 40 years old. Many were alone following the breakdown of long-standing relationships. The majority were not in paid employment and nearly all were living in poverty, dependent on benefits for their income. Most of the families were rather socially isolated, having few people on whom they could depend in social, emotional and

practical ways. While they often lived quite close to their families, they did not have especially strong links with them.

High levels of chronic physical, stress-related illness, and of anxiety and depression, were characteristic of the parents in the study. The following comment was made by a 28-year-old mother, with two children aged seven and nine, living in an inner-city bedsit, and waiting to be rehoused:

> 'It is hard on the children since he [husband] left. I get very low sometimes and a bit ratty, and there's nowhere much for them to play. [The short-term break scheme] is a godsend; it gives me a break and they have a lot of fun. I'm glad to see them again.'

Parents expressed a strong commitment to their children and to the quality of their lives. Short-term care was most often sought for relief from the day-to-day demands of bringing up children in social and economic deprivation, which made the task considerably more difficult. A break for themselves, while knowing that the children were well cared for, was what most parents hoped for from the arrangements. The children's enjoyment of the visits was an important but complicated matter for parents, since it also brought worries about the possibility of children feeling dissatisfied with home. One parent commented 'I was very nervous at first, in case Stuart thought I didn't want him, and I wondered if [the carer] would cope. He'd never been away before. He had a great time. In fact, I wondered if he liked it better there.'

Families thought highly of the services they received, and commented particularly on the *quality* of the work of the carers, their approachability and practical sensitivity, as this comment illustrates: 'Well, they were really good. They never looked down on me – never. She was sort of ordinary but special. I always felt like Becky's mum and I knew I could always talk to her.'

Often, the greatest difficulties were associated with the earliest contact with the agency, in reaching the point where parents were considered 'eligible' for short-term breaks. They frequently felt they had to be 'desperate' before help would be offered: 'I saw three different social workers before anyone really listened. I said I'd murder him if they didn't give me some help – but I didn't want to lose him, I've never hurt him. Then she told me about it [short-term breaks]. It's been brilliant.'

Ongoing support and advice from social workers was generally much valued. Parents worried a great deal that seeking outside help may undermine their confidence and coping ability, that needing support will be seen as indicative of failure as parents, that their children may feel rejected by them or prefer the care they receive elsewhere. Parents usually found social workers approachable, helpful, honest and reliable in the process of making the arrangements and in their meetings afterwards: one parent stated of the social worker

> 'Oh! she really did seem to *understand*. She offered me the right amount of help at the right time – any different and it would have taken away my confidence. I did worry that they would think I was a bad parent.'

Children's views of short-term breaks

The study also involved observations of and discussions with children between the ages of 1 and 15 years. Those who were old enough to talk to us about their experiences of short-term care were usually unrestrained and articulate in doing so, and some of the younger children could make use of guided play – usually structured around telling a story about a visit to the carer family – to give a sense of their feelings about the breaks. All the interviews were enriched by the opportunity to observe the children in their homes with *their* parents, and occasionally with their carers. Talking to parents about their understanding of the child's experience was also useful, particularly with regard to the interdependence of children's and parents' needs. The children were usually quite clear about the arrangements, and most had a good understanding of the reasons for them. Most of the children saw the purpose of the arrangements being first and foremost to give their *parent* a break, and this was very often accompanied by an understanding that this would help the parent to continue to take care of the child. While a few of the children accurately saw the primary reason for the arrangements being to give themselves a break from stressful circumstances at home, the greatest number felt the breaks to be beneficial to both parent and child. One eight-year-old girl commented 'It's so my mum can have a rest and maybe go out a bit, but it's lovely going there, once I got used to it.'

Children from families of all sizes received short-term breaks and it was fairly unusual for only one child in a family to have time away.

Sometimes younger children went and older ones did not, and occasionally an older child had breaks if younger siblings required a good
deal of time and attention. Where only one child in a family received
short-term accommodation, amongst the older children, these children
more frequently saw themselves as the primary focus of the arrangements, either because they had a particular need for respite from family
stresses, or for individual attention which was in short supply. Occasionally this raised some conflict between brothers and sisters, for
example, because those who did not go to the carers felt that those who
did were getting something rather special and desirable. Where large
sibling groups needed short-term care, arrangements were often made
with two carer families, with the children making two smaller groups.

All of the children found that talking about the arrangements, as
part of the preparation process, helped them to think about what the
visits might be like, and what might be difficult for them. Without a
doubt, however, preparatory visits to the carer's home were the most
important factor in reassuring the children and in helping them to feel
less worried about being away from home. Asked what helped to
reassure him about the arrangements, one six-year-old boy responded
'It was when I saw the bed that was meant for me that I knew it was
alright'. This little boy had assumed he would have to share a bed, since
this was what he was accustomed to at home. Children commented
again and again on the sense of reassurance they had from meeting the
carer family, from seeing the home and their place in it, and of having
an idea of family routine, which nevertheless took account of them and
their special needs and wishes. A seven-year-old boy commented:

> 'We went to tea, me and Jenny, and Mum. We had sandwiches and
> cake. Only I don't like egg, I was really worried. I thought, what
> would I do if it was only what I didn't like? But she asked me –
> don't you like egg? Then she asked if I'd like cheese instead, and
> what else did I specially not like?'

Despite the generally excellent and invaluable preparation, homesickness was nevertheless a universal problem for the children. One child
aged ten remarked 'Oh! it was hard, it's not the same. You can't just go
to the cupboard and get something to eat when you like. I felt lonely.
Now it's great, now I'm used to it', while another, asked if she missed
being at home, replied 'Well, no. Maybe. I did miss Mum... and
David... and Joey... and Nan... and...' A boy aged five was asked if he

worried about being away from home. He answered 'Oh, yes! I couldn't think where she [Mum] was and if she was alright.'

Most of the children found it helpful to know they could telephone home, if this was possible, or that the parent would telephone the carer's home at a certain time. The majority felt their carers would understand and be sympathetic to their feelings, and would be 'there' if needed. It seemed important for the children to feel reassured of the carer's concern, but that they took the lead in seeking the carer. On the whole, children found it most helpful to have some private time to recover their equilibrium, with background support from the carer. A nine-year-old girl commented 'I like to be by myself, and think a bit, when I'm sad. She [carer] knows though.'

Finally, what children enjoyed and valued, and commented on most frequently, was the *quality* of care they received. The kindness and consideration they experienced from the carers, and the opportunity to relax and play, were much more frequently mentioned than material advantages, as this comment indicates: 'They're alright... kind, you know. And they play with me.'

Most of the children talked quite easily to parents and sometimes to social workers about their thoughts and feelings regarding the arrangements being made for them, and so were able to participate in both consultation and review: 'I was glad to talk about it. I was a bit surprised when they asked me, you know. Well, I thought, I have to go, don't I? But she really did ask what *I* thought, and what *I* wanted.'

The decision to use short-term breaks
The decision to use short-term breaks is usually a complex one, reached after a good deal of heart-searching. Parents and children have worries about what it will entail and what it may mean for their future as a family.

Parents sometimes worry that children may see the request for short-term breaks as a 'letting go' of caring responsibility, and that other people, including professionals, may perceive it this way. They also worry that the experience of spending time in a home where life seems more fortunate and less stressful may lead their children to prefer this home and these parents. Not least, parents sometimes have difficult feelings of envy, when their children receive the care they themselves might like to have had. These anxieties are difficult to voice, particularly if parents feel that such fears will influence how they are seen and the service they will receive. When these worries are openly discussed, the stability and the success of the arrangements undoubtedly benefit. Similarly, families find openness in other aspects of discussion and consultation invaluable. Parents and children must have a clear idea of what short-term care is and what it is not. Families need to be fully informed about the possibilities and limitations of resources, about the role of the agency and of professional workers, about the aims of the plan and the purpose of any other parts of the 'package'. They need to know, as far as possible, what to expect and to be enabled to explore these ideas in the context of their own perceived needs and those of their children.

Creating links between parents, children and carers

When making arrangements for children, many things will need to be thought about and it is important that *all* factors are considered and that no particular issue should assume overall importance. Different issues will be important for different children or in relation to the same child at different times (Department of Health 1991b).

Where there are important factors relating to ethnic origin, cultural background and religion, linking parents and child with a carer family from a similar background seems likely to make the best provision for the child's needs and welfare. For some children in the study, the continuity of these important dimensions of their own family life *was* the most important consideration in making short-term arrangements. There were times when the direct possibilities for meeting the ethnic, cultural and religious needs of children were limited because there were no carers available from similar groups. When this did happen, the family needed to know that this was so, and be helped to make the best decision for the child in the light of the limitations. In practice, carer families with different cultural, ethnic or religious backgrounds *did* sensitively understand and make provision for special and important aspects of the child's life which lay outside their own family experience.

Sometimes other factors took precedence for the child and the family. Keeping other links – those with friends, school or neighbourhood – or finding a carer family who could take all of a sibling group was sometimes more important. The essential thing is that the decision rests with the family and is made with them, on the basis of informed discussion.

A degree of common ground in culture, lifestyle and life experience seems to ease communication and transitions between the two homes. Each *family* needs to have sufficient understanding and acceptance of the other to find enough common ground for the *child* to feel comfortable. The values of parents and carers need to be explored and discussed in relation to everyday issues such as discipline, rewards, eating, playing, bedtime, pocket money and the like. The guiding principle is to *safeguard continuity* in the child's life, as far as possible, and to let the child know that the arrangements are being made by adults who have thought about his needs and wishes, and who have taken the trouble to know about him.

Some key elements in successful arrangements

The success of arrangements needs to be thought about in several different but related ways. Whether or not the family stays together is clearly the most crucial determinant of success in the long term. In the more immediate sense, other aspects can be 'successful' or not, in their own right. Have the stays been enjoyable for the child? Have the stays helped the child with other aspects of his/her life? Was the child able to make his thoughts and feelings clear to the adults making the arrangements? Were these taken into account? Similarly, one needs to ask questions about the quality of the parents' experiences. What were the characteristics of the 'working' relationship with social workers and with carers? How well informed were parents? How easy was it to put forward their thoughts and wishes? Were these taken properly into account? Did parents feel respected and responsible in the consultation and decision-making processes? These are interim but also independent measures of success. Overall, they are fundamentally important in their own right, and they are undoubtedly linked to the long-term success or failure of the intervention. In this research, the critical factors identified as being related to successful outcomes include the quality of partnership between parent, agency and carer, the quality of consultation for parent and for the child, the preparation of child and of parent, and the personal qualities of the carer.

Partnership and consultation

'Partnership' implies an equal and informed meeting of those concerned with making decisions. It is important to bear in mind that the participants have different roles and different levels of power in the process of discussion and negotiation, and will be affected by different constraints. In making short-term accommodation arrangements, the participants may include several social workers – one for the scheme and possibly one for the family and another for the carer. Others may be involved if they have a role in the welfare of this particular family. So far, so good. All come with a 'common' purpose in mind – meeting the needs of the children within their family – but that purpose may mean rather different things for each participant. The short-term accommodation study found that parents and social workers frequently brought questions and concerns to consultation which reflected their different roles, and which sometimes seemed difficult to address directly. For parents, these issues related to 'pitching the request at the right level', so that difficulties were recognised but not overestimated, so that supportive and appropriate help was offered, rather than too much or none at all. Social workers, on the other hand, were often concerned to know if the level of stress in the family implied the need for more formal involvement – were there more difficulties than met the eye? The *meaningful* consultation of parents called for careful consideration of family circumstances in an atmosphere of sufficient trust to enable parents to speak freely and honestly. While there may always be a degree of inevitable asymmetry between the participants, this need not preclude partnership, if parents feel they are listened to with respect and without prejudgment, and that information is honestly given. The key elements of constructive partnership include the *recognition* of differences and constraints, and a readiness to acknowledge and build on the strengths of the family. It requires the giving and receiving of information with honesty and respect. It means making sure that the process is clear and thoughtfully planned, including the timing and location of meetings, the timescale, the use of jargon-free language, and accountability to the parents as a *primary* responsibility.

Going outside the family for help is a complicated business which may temporarily undermine the confidence of parent and child, or the integrity of the family. There are points at which the arrangements may falter, or even founder, if consultation and participation in making decisions are observed in the letter but not the spirit of the process.

Opportunities for work which strengthens families are too valuable to be lost.

Consulting children

The need to identify and take into account the wishes and feelings of the children raises important questions. How best to 'consult' children? How to give them information without burdening them with decision-making? When and to what extent must the information from the child be supplemented by information from other people? When are children mature enough, that is, when do they have enough knowledge of the world, to make informed decisions about their own welfare? How will the worker resolve differences between the child and the parents, or between the child and herself? When the social worker talks to the child – how does she relate what she perceives of the child to what is normal for children of that age? How much does the social worker understand of how the child thinks and what the child's expectations and hopes of adults might be? How can the social worker use ways other than talking to help the child express his wishes and feelings? Each social worker will have to ensure that he or she has the necessary practical and theoretical skills to hold a conversation with children which has meaning. The constellation of each child's characteristics and circumstances will have its special and individual significance.

Preparing for placements

Short-term accommodation is, in one sense, just a brief break from home. However, most children and many parents are not always certain what it will mean, and they are sometimes very worried indeed about what it might be like. Children and parents also worry about each other while they are apart, however welcome the break may be. Some anticipation of what it may feel like to be worried and homesick is helpful for children and their parents. If it is particularly difficult to think about these worries, it may help to describe the feelings that children and parents commonly do have about being somewhere strange. It is also important to prepare parents and children for the complicated feelings of readjustment which both may feel when the child returns home. Parents and children need to hear about the carer family early in the discussion process. If a choice is possible, information and time to think about options must be offered, too. If choice is restricted, the reasons for this need to be clearly stated. This is a time when questions and worries can be sensitively explored, and then followed by visits to the carer family's home, which helps to ground worries in reality. These are vitally important, for parent and child. Most parents and children found two visits helpful, with the second being more informal, perhaps an invitation to tea and to spend some time with the carer's children. Children said over and over again, how reassuring they found these visits. Meeting the carer family and seeing where they would sleep and eat and play helped to lessen their anxiety about being away from home. Parents are similarly reassured by such visits, and by feeling they are welcome in the carer's home, and respected as the child's parent. Clear arrangements for contact between the two homes during the visit are very important, but the vital link for the child's peace of mind is the sense of trust and respect between parent and carer.

The short-term carers

For children and parents, the personal qualities of the carers were *vital* to the success of arrangements. Steady, practical kindness, thoughtfulness, reliability and the 'individual' time given by carers were the qualities children valued. For parents, it was the experience of being treated as a responsible adult and parent, and the warmth and support of their contact with the carer family. Somehow, the quietly stated emphasis on a 'working relationship' with parents translated into an endorsement of parental strengths which also allowed the child to benefit from this second family experience without feeling unduly divided.

There is much to be said about the selection, training and support of short-term carers (Sellick 1994), but here an attempt will be made to capture the particular qualities which were so valued by children and their parents. While short-term carers frequently choose to work in this way because it fits in with their other family and work commitments, they also expressed a firm commitment to work which helped keep families together. Some carers were very perceptive about the difficulties which user families had, in part because they had weathered their own troubled times, as this comment illustrates:

> 'I was on my own for a while, with three kids. You know, it is hard... there doesn't seem to be an end to it. I had a really good

friend, she could just sort of, take the weight off me sometimes. It made the difference, it really did.'

Some spoke of the value of their own support network, and this seemed to highlight a sensitive awareness of the lack of family-based support for many user parents: 'We appreciate how much parents miss being able to be sure of someone to help out, someone to talk to – we couldn't do our work without the back up of our families.'

It was noticeable that carers who enjoyed and saw a special value in short-term breaks frequently had previous experience which naturally included a real working relationship with parents, most notably childminding. While carers regarded the child as the most important focus of their work, this was set in a fundamental commitment to the welfare of the family, and to working with parents. One carer observed 'The regular stays give Mum a break – she's very isolated. But Jenny [the child] is too independent – she needs to be a little girl before it's too late.'

Working with parents was felt to be both rewarding and difficult, but carers seemed able to accept and respect parental responsibility and authority.

In general, the hardest part of giving short-term breaks was coping with the 'comings and goings' between two homes, and in supporting but not supplanting the role of the parent: 'You sometimes feel you've just got them right, when it's time for them to go again. At the end of the day, though, they go home – where they should be.'

Conclusions

The research into the use of short-term breaks as a support for children from families in need has highlighted the following points:

- it *can* help keep families together
- short-term breaks are highly valued by families
- children enjoy short-term breaks for time to relax and play
- children need to talk about their experiences and benefit from doing so
- it must be recognised that homesickness and worries about parents affect most children while away
- children value the personal, caring qualities of the carers

- family support services should be targeted *before* crisis occurs
- short-term breaks are helpful where long-standing difficulties of poverty, isolation and lack of support are high on the list of family problems
- some families have experienced many disruptions
- parents worry that intervention may undermine family relationships and family integrity
- service providers should be aware that some parents may have high levels of physical and mental stress-related illness
- preparation for child and for parent is vital
- contact and co-operation between user and carer homes are essential for children's well-being
- short-term carers need to see working with parents as a crucial and integral part of their task
- short-term breaks work well when parents feel acknowledged and respected as parents
- good training and support of carers is central to successful short-term care
- good short-term care takes time, effort and money
- service providers should ensure that colleagues in other agencies know about the use of short-term breaks
- good, clear information about short-term accommodation services needs to be widely available in the community.

References

Aldgate, J. (1993) 'Respite care for children – an old remedy in a new package.' In P. Marsh and J. Tresiliotis (eds) *Prevention and Reunification in Child Care*. London: Batsford.

Aldgate, J., Pratt, R. and Duggan, M. (1989) 'Using care away from home to prevent family breakdown.' *Adoption and Fostering 13, 2, 32–37*.

Aldgate, J., Bradley, M. and Hawley, D. (1995) *Report to the Department of Health on the Use of Short-term Accommodation in the Prevention of Long-term Family Breakdown*. London: HMSO.

Bradley, M. and Aldgate, J. (1995) *A Practice Guide to the Use of Short-term Accommodation*. London: HMSO.

Department of Health (1989a) *The Children Act 1989*. London: HMSO.

Department of Health (1989b) *An Introduction to the Children Act*. London: HMSO.

Department of Health (1991a) *The Children Act 1989, Guidance and Regulations. Vol 2, Family Support, Day Care and Educational Provision for Young Children*. London: HMSO.

Department of Health (1991b) *The Children Act 1989, Guidance and Regulations. Vol 3, Family Placements*. London: HMSO.

Gibbons, J. (ed) (1992) *The Children Act and Family Support: Principles into Practice*. London: HMSO.

Ignatieff, M. (1992) *The Needs of Strangers*. London: Hogarth.

National Council of Voluntary Child Care Organisations (1991) *The Children Act and Children's Needs: Make it the Answer – Not the Problem*. London: In Need Implementation Group.

Sellick, C. (1994) *Supporting Short-term Carers*. Aldershot: Avebury.

Chapter 8

Home and Away
People with Dementia and their Carers
Carole Archibald

Introduction

A famous Glasgow geriatrician once gave a recipe for being taken care of in old age: 'Have children; have daughters and don't argue with them.' There is more than a grain of truth in this homily. With current estimates of three-quarters of a million people in the United Kingdom having dementia by the year 2021 (Alzheimer's Disease Society 1992), the implications for services are massive. Studies show the family is the best asset the country has in caring for people in the community.

Community care has traditionally been care mainly by families, often female members (Badger and Cameron 1990, Horrowitz 1985). Levin, Moriarty and Gorbach (1993), in their study involving 287 people and their carers, reported that 80 per cent of the carers were spouses or daughters, with women outnumbering men as carers by three to one. Carers have received support in different measures from the statutory services. The aim of introducing residential respite care in the 1950s was to aid the continuation of this arrangement. This dovetails nicely with the 1990s policy of community care. However, a note of caution needs to be sounded.

While the principle of keeping older people in the community is generally accepted, in that this is where most people tend to want to be and most carers want to continue caring, this is not universal (Nolan and Grant 1992). Some people would choose not to care (Gilhooley 1986), some carers would like more flexible and more appropriate respite (Melzer 1990, Nolan and Grant 1992) and some would simply like more (Levin *et al.* 1989, 1994).

Although very altruistic, helping people to care also makes sound economic sense. However, there are difficulties. Care in the community is not economic in every case. The cost for those people needing intensive care in the community is not small compared to the alternatives (Melzer 1990). This particularly applies to people with dementia. When confronted with economic reality, altruism might need to be discarded. Residential care, in some cases, will be the most likely option. Again, as Levin *et al.* (1993, p.1) assert, 'respite services at current levels cannot be presented as an alternative to residential care'.

The term 'respite' itself is not without conflict. Increasingly the preference is for terms such as 'short breaks' or 'shared care' to be used. The term 'respite' has negative connotations. It suggests that the task of caring is burdensome, a load carers need to be relieved of. However, many carers, health groups and social work staff use this term, particularly with reference to residential respite. It is also the term used in much of the literature reviewed for this chapter. As Lindsay *et al.* (1993) state, the term persists. This chapter will for the most part focus on residential respite care and so the term 'respite' will be used here.

Reviewing current literature on short breaks or respite care for people with dementia, terminology is not the only difficulty to emerge. There are also paradoxes with regard to the role of respite in community care. It was set up originally to help carers continue to care. While the literature tends to be inconclusive regarding this particular outcome, most studies point to respite as being a pertinent and positive factor in the care process, yet it is a diminishing resource. The closure of long-stay wards where traditionally many people with dementia received respite care, the varying cost of many local authority respite beds, and the lack and cost of provision in the private sector, are all having an impact. Both underprovision and lack of service uptake are reported.

The underprovision of respite care is not a recent phenomenon. In 1987, Webb reported that, while respite care had increased in response to demand, there was still insufficient provision. It was estimated that for each respite scheme there was a potential user population of approximately 6500 carers, depending on geography. Levin *et al.* (1994) and Hedley (1991) also report limited respite provision. This underprovision now seems at odds with the emphasis on community care. The dearth of hard data on how services function (Allen 1983, Brook and Jestice 1986, Lindsay *et al.* 1993) is also at odds with the current emphasis on accountability. This is particularly pertinent in the field of dementia.

The under-use of respite services is noted by Brodaty and Gresham (1992) in Australia, and Lawton, Brody and Saperstein (1989) in the US. In response to the under-use of respite care, Kosloski and Montgomery (1993) looked at how perceptions of respite services can be used as predictors of utilisation of the service. The research looked at three specific features: usefulness, quality and convenience of the service. These features will be used in the present chapter when considering the carer's perspective.

Many questions need to be addressed. In all advanced societies, the rising costs of health care, coupled with an increasingly elderly population, is forcing the issue of respite care to the fore. Britain is no different. However, as Lindsay *et al.* (1993, p.4) state, 'respite is on the agenda of a large number of people, but at the top of very few of those agendas'. This will have to change. Respite is viewed generally as an essential part of community care, but it must match the needs of both receivers and caregivers if it is to demonstrate efficacy (Brodaty and Gresham 1992).

Respite care can be described as any service which provides temporary relief for the caregiver (Brodaty and Gresham 1992). It can take the form of domiciliary sitter services, daycare or residential respite: 'home and away' in effect. It can and often is a combination of all three. It can be planned or emergency. The time can vary from hours to days to months. The location, amount and type is dependent on a variety of factors. Respite is a moveable feast. It has to be if it purports to meet the needs of people with dementia and their carers. But does it? Levin *et al.* (1993) reported that respite services were given in standard amounts at standard intervals; for example, most residential care was often for 14 days. When the issues are teased out, it becomes apparent that respite needs for this group of people are manifold, complex and not without conflict. Nevertheless, little specialist provision exists.

People with dementia tend to be cared for in mainstream provision within the existing framework of health or social work services (Levin *et al.* 1993). Although there has been a mushrooming of specialist domiciliary (Lindsay *et al.* 1993) and daycare for people with dementia, many still receive care from non-specialist service providers such as district nurses with large caseloads and limited time, and home helps who work set hours and have little training in dementia care. The home-help service in some areas is developing a more flexible provision, with staff working evenings and weekends. Some have received training, allowing their role to be extended to provide a range of duties including bathing and toiletting. This has to be applauded. It limits the number of people going into the house of a confused person with dementia.

In Scotland, Lindsay *et al.* (1993) found that 34 per cent of residential respite for people with dementia was within residential homes and 66 per cent within hospital services. At the time of their report, there was no family-based provision. In the case of residential care, only nine schemes provided beds specifically for people with dementia and, of these, just one was a 'respite only' scheme. Allen (1983) highlights an important difficulty in admitting a person with dementia to non-specialist residential homes: the fact that established residents may find disturbed newcomers disruptive. The person with dementia may also have difficulties coping.

These findings give pause for thought. How do they relate to the concerns of this age: the patient's charter, standard setting and quality assurance? If the key issue in quality assurance is the assumption that the service user, rather than the service provider is central (Social Services Inspectorate 1993), then what of their voice? There are two groups of people, at least, who have needs in dementia care: the carer and the person with dementia. Where possible, both sets of needs have to be taken cognisance of. Which services provide a positive experience for both? What of issues relating to equal opportunities? What also are the needs of service providers? These issues are topical and need to be considered in the light of the community care legislation and the 'modernisation' of the health service. If the rationale for respite care is helping the person remain in the community for as long as possible, does respite care prevent admission to long-term care? This chapter will explore research findings in all these areas, beginning with the carers.

Carers

Since the rationale for providing respite care has been to allow carers to go on caring, essentially to prevent long-term admission, then there is a need to examine, as many have done (Levin *et al.* 1989, 1994, Gilhooley 1986), who are these carers and what impact has respite care had on them? Has respite delayed admission to long-term care? Are carers seen as a bulwark against the increasing numbers of people suffering from dementia, making demands on services? How are they viewed by service providers and how does this affect the allocation of respite care?

Service providers have varying perceptions of carers. This is an important point, because the way in which they are viewed influences the services they receive (Twigg 1989). Carers can be seen as a resource, a co-worker, or a client. Twigg (1992) adds a fourth model, the superseded carer, where the person being cared for either gains independence or, more relevantly here, enters care.

So who are the people who care? Generally, family members tend to be the main carers. Levin *et al.*'s (1989) findings showed 85 per cent of principal supporters were either the older person's spouse (41%) or their children (44%). Of the 85 per cent of carers mentioned, two-thirds were women. Others have acknowledged this massive contribution by women (Qureshi and Walker 1989).

But does gender matter? Is it of significance in the caring situation? The immediate significance is that of demographic change. The sexual work revolution (Hochschild 1989) has resulted in increasing numbers of women in the work place. In Britain, the demise of male-dominated industries and the rise of service industries, which can be major employers of women, could have far-reaching implications for the availability of carers. Women tend to combine both paid and unpaid roles (Parker 1985), to the impairment of their health (Jones and Peters 1992, Brody 1981). There is evidence to suggest that wives especially pay a high physical and psychological price such as depression, stress and drug use (Brody 1981, Zarit, Todd and Zarit 1986). Brody (1981) describes daughter carers as 'women in the middle', with demands not only being made by parents, but also by husbands and children.

The literature points to men and women using different models of care. Male carers generally tend to use the task-orientated model, getting through the tasks in the most efficient manner. They tend to purchase the services of other women for housework and other physical chores (Pruchno and Resch 1989). It is interesting to note that one study found that having a home help lessened the likelihood of an older person's admission to residential care, but only if their supporter was a man (Levin *et al.* 1989).

In her study of gender differences in dementia management, Corcoran (1992) discusses the male task-orientated approach and also the societal view and expectations of the woman's caring role, involving high levels of self-sacrifice. Women tend to spend more time per week in care tasks. Wives are less likely than their husbands to receive due acknowledgement, as it is an expectation that they adopt this role. For instance, Badger and Cameron (1990) found that wives were less likely than husbands to receive community nursing services or home helps. This relative absence of community support resulted in increased respite admissions.

Are women given more respite? Are they more accepting of respite than men? Who tends to avail themselves of respite? Levin *et al.* (1989) found that daughters were particularly likely to use the service, unlike spouses over 75 years of age. The authors also pointed to the finding that respite care was often provided when some supporters would have preferred long-term care. A prior link with professionals was a key factor in obtaining a break.

What do carers want?

Overwhelmingly, respite care of all types has been described as valuable (Brodaty and Gresham 1992) and often indispensable (Levin *et al.* 1994), although some studies show that residential respite failed to show an observable improvement in the carer's emotional well-being (Homer and Gilleard 1994). Respite care in many instances provides the only chance to relax, see the family or catch up on household chores (Berry, Zarit and Rabatin 1991). Home-based services are particularly appreciated (Levin *et al.* 1994).

Carers of people with dementia are not a homogeneous group. Their needs can differ widely (Berry *et al.* 1991). It follows therefore that respite services need to be varied and flexible to meet this diverse need. Time and again it emerges that carers want flexibility, accessibility and involvement in the design and delivery of the service (Lindsay *et al.* 1993). They want information, and a menu of services so they can make an informed choice. They want reliable and sensitive services where staff are trained and thus have an understanding of issues. They want a service where the person with dementia has their needs met (Hedley 1991). The services also, topically, need to be affordable.

Respite should be seen as a package. Berry *et al.* (1991) suggest that, when first considering respite, the timing of breaks is important, as well as educating the carer about respite and the use of free time. Carers often need to be taught to think about how they can best look after themselves. This is something which is often overlooked. 'Follow up' also needs to be considered, looking at how the person fares when they return home and, as the dementia progresses, monitoring changes and offering interventions accordingly.

The carers interviewed in Levin *et al.*'s study (1989) highlighted the importance of a thorough preparation for respite care. At a basic level, they meant simply knowing which residential home the person was to go to; where possible, a prior visit would have been helpful. They would have preferred a two-way exchange of information, with staff taking note of the carer's knowledge of the individual, and informing the carer about the person's progress. In the 1994 study, Levin *et al.* found that the provision of residential respite was targeted, with those more severely dependent and behaviourally disturbed being offered the service. It seems that respite care is offered as a palliative when the carer is already under stress, rather than being used to prevent stress.

Issues for carers

If, as is suggested, most carers want to continue caring (Levin *et al.* 1994, Hedley 1991), then the way forward has to be towards early intervention and support, to avoid exploitation and consequently high morbidity rates in carers. Even with some service provision, studies have shown adverse health consequences for carers (Eagles and Gilleard 1984, Pruchno and Resch 1989). Respite is an important unmet need expressed by carers in several studies (Crossman, London and Barry 1981, Equal Opportunities Commission 1980). In Levin *et al.*'s (1989) initial interviews, three out of four carers had never had respite care; most had never been offered it.

If it is reasoned that respite care is instrumental in keeping people in the community by delaying or rationing long-term care, then it is important to know why some people do not receive it or fail to take advantage of it.

Underprovision

The Scottish Health Board Survey (Jacques 1994) established that some health services did not provide respite beds for people with dementia. The reasons varied from the increased demand for long-term beds, to fear that carers might short circuit the long-term waiting list by refusing to take their relative home following a respite admission. Increasingly, with the closure of long-stay wards, respite beds will be an even scarcer resource. At present, the debate continues as to whether social or health services are responsible for respite provision for people with dementia, with the private and voluntary organisations on the fringe of events. The emphasis in the health service is now on acute care, assessment and rehabilitation.

Respite care is seen more and more as the responsibility of the social services rather than health. However, Lindsay *et al.* (1993) noted that respite care in some hospitals appears under the heading of 'assessment'. Anecdotally, it would seem to be the case that some ward staff are providing respite care under the guise of assessment.

The move to the private sector will inevitably influence the availability of respite care. If America is seen as the main role model, then respite care will increasingly come to mean daycare or sitter services – respite in the person's own home, in effect, rather than institutional respite which, because of the uncertainties in filling bed spaces, tends not to be profitable. There are also complications in the organisation of respite as opposed to long-term beds.

Inappropriate or unsuitable respite care
Maxwell (1984) suggests the quality of a service can be considered in terms of access, effectiveness for the individual, equity and relevance to need. Kosloski and Montgomery (1993) emphasise that quality of care and the overall usefulness of the service need to be taken into account. They found that even if the service is free or heavily subsidised, if it is inconvenient to use, low quality or simply not useful, then there will be a reduced uptake. Haley and Pardo (1989) suggest that the need for respite might be greatest in the 'middle' stages of the disease when wandering, aggression and other challenging behaviours are present. If this is the case, then where will people be referred if there is little specialist provision?

When respite care is provided in hospitals, there may be very disturbed people in the ward. The whole situation is unacceptable to the carer, especially when their relative is younger or retains some insight or is less severely affected. In spite of these disadvantages, in hospital the service is free of charge, and it can provide an opportunity for a medical assessment. Some carers find a medical/professional environment more acceptable. The role of hospitals is significant and, as Lindsay *et al.* (1993) report, considerable anxiety has been expressed by carers at the reduction in beds without a corresponding increase of services in the community.

The difficulties around respite care provided by residential or private homes arise from lack of specialist provision for people with challenging behaviour. Sometimes staff are not trained in the needs of this client group. The building may not afford a safe environment for people who might wander. These factors can act as barriers to the home accepting people with dementia, or carers may refuse the offer of respite care in the home because it is deemed unsuitable.

In terms of service relevance, a pertinent question concerns the appropriateness of respite services to minority ethnic groups and younger people with dementia. These two groups are not well served (Cox and McLennan 1994).

Heptinstall (1989), discussing daycare and older people generally, considers mixed race day centres and the possibility that racist practices or attitudes might cause black people not to attend. Mixed centres could be seen as inappropriate. In a society where racism is endemic, if a separate day centre makes people feel more comfortable, why not have a separate centre and domiciliary services, similar to Jewish or Asian centres? The main point seems to be that service providers should not make assumptions. There is a constant need to keep in touch with users locally and nationally to find out what people really want. This is equally true for people with dementia and their carers from different cultures.

Poonia and Ward (1990) suggest three issues for carers which need to be considered: information and communication, concerns about how their relatives will be looked after, and the availability of black carers and professionals. Although this paper looks at carers of black children, the issues are pertinent to carers of black people with dementia.

Carers of younger people with dementia, whether black or white, are poorly served. Hedley (1991), in his survey of carers, found concern that the needs of this group were not being met. Services tend to be linked in with provision for older people, which was seen as inappropriate, with few specialist services for those who were younger.

Research points to carers tending to accept or be offered residential respite when dementia is already well developed (Brodaty and Gresham 1992, Levin *et al.* 1993). Most carers cite flexibility as a very important component of a quality service, yet most places, whether hospital or residential homes, offer a two-week break which does not suit everyone. Many package holidays start mid week, for example. Respite care is often provided from Saturday to Saturday.

Family-based care is discussed by Levin *et al.* (1993) as a positive way forward for some people. Whilst this model is more homely and less confusing than a large institution, it still involves the confused and disorientated person being moved and having to make adjustments. Again, this kind of respite does not appeal to all carers, with some showing a preference for 'professional' care. Several studies point to the need for choice – a menu of different options so that carers and the person with dementia can make an informed choice.

There are a few schemes which offer a paid worker who will stay in the client's own home for a week or more. If paid on an hourly rate, it would be very expensive for someone to stay in the person's home over a period of a week or more on a 24-hour basis.

It has emerged from some studies that carers want more 'in home' respite care. George (1986) reported that 'in home' respite was useful in that it saved carers the task of having to get the person ready on time for daycare. The main benefit of a sitter service is that it is least disruptive to the person with dementia, although it can mean the carer has to go out of the house to obtain a break. For some carers, the sitter becomes a friend and confidante. Sitter services tend to be less rigid in the hours they offer and are another way of giving the carer a break for a short period of time. They are often complementary, or can be an entry point, to more mainstream daycare provision or indeed residential respite care (Levin *et al.* 1993). Sitter services can be particularly useful when the person with dementia either refuses, or is too physically frail to attend daycare, or when behavioural problems means that daycare is not an option.

There are many sitter services around the country, although under-provision and lack of resources often mean that provision has to be rationed. Levin *et al.* (1993) found that, while carers were greatly appreciative of the sitter service and would have liked more, three-quarters received this service once a week or less. The cost of commercial sitter services is seen as too restrictive for regular use.

Daycare, provided by health, social and increasingly voluntary services, where the person is transported from their home, is one of the main sources of community care for people with dementia. It is the service that people with dementia are most likely to use, providing carers with a regular weekly break. Good quality daycare is increasingly geared to stimulating the person with dementia, improving their quality of life, while at the same time giving carers a break. The unpredictability of transport has been cited as a difficulty and the rigid times of daycare is another drawback. Daycare tends to be 10.00am-3.00pm Monday-Friday, with people being offered on average two days per week (Badger and Cameron 1990). What carers wanted when asked was flexible (this word is cited time and again in the literature) day and evening care, and sitter services with day and evening flexibility. In one study, some carers had to persist in trying to get care arrangements they wanted, despite repeated professional assessments and prescriptions of inappropriate care (Melzer 1990). Greater variety, more flexibility and identifying a gap between regular relief and annual or crisis admissions are called for (Levin *et al.* 1989, Nolan and Grant .1992).

Guilt

Guilt seems to be a major barrier to using residential respite care. Residential respite is not usually in the interests of the person with dementia although the opportunity for an assessment over 24 hours, or more social contacts, have some benefit. However, it is again the only break that gives the carer a real rest from caring. It is not without its price. Often, because of feelings of guilt, carers only use respite as a last resort (Tyler 1989). It does not help that staff often seem to be unaware of the guilt feelings carers experience and so little is done to alleviate them (Twigg 1989). Pearson (1988) documents that 50 per cent of carers felt sad or lonely, 20 per cent guilty, and 20 per cent reported criticisms from friends and relatives for allowing relief admissions in the first place.

Refusal

Carers sometimes refuse the offer of respite care because they feel that paid staff cannot provide the personal care they can. They often feel their own hard-won and expert knowledge is not taken note of by staff (Bowers 1987). Nolan and Grant (1992) add that failure to take account of this knowledge resulted in perceived inadequacy in any form of institutional care. Carers are also anxious about the possible deterioration of their relative (Levin *et al.* 1989, 1993). However, the refusal of respite care is not just the prerogative of the carer. The person with dementia also can refuse to accept admission. This raises the subject of carer/client conflict, and the rights and needs of the person with dementia versus those of the carer. Who in effect is the client (Badger and Cameron 1990)?

Often people with dementia are referred to services because of the needs of carers. However, anxiety about facing new situations, using services which are not geared to their needs and routine, or simply a wish to remain in their own home and near their carer because that is where they are happiest, might lead people with dementia to refuse a 'holiday'. This is the dilemma which faces professionals. Sometimes it is resolved only by crisis admission of the person with dementia to long-term care following the breakdown of the carer's health.

Where services are geared to simply offering the carer a break and not taking into account the needs of the person with dementia, carers might have difficulty accepting them. They may, as a consequence, refuse offers of respite care (Badger and Cameron 1990). The person with dementia will be considered next.

The person with dementia

'My mind is like a dark thunderstorm.'

This quotation comes from Alice Zilonka, a person with dementia (Alzheimer's Disease Society 1992). It gives a useful insight of how dementia must feel to the person with the disease. The feelings of people with dementia about service provision have not been sought until recently. The main emphasis has been on the needs of carers. There is an increasing awareness that the needs of the person have to be taken into account. Lindow and Morris (1994, p.2) state that 'Community care organisations often find it easier to consult with people identified as "carers" rather than with service users themselves.' This is particularly the case with people with dementia.

Sperlinger and McAuslane (1994), in their pilot study to obtain the views of people with dementia on services, acknowledge the difficulties, but show that with patience and skill it can be achieved. They point to the creative ideas that have been used in the field of learning disability compared to attempts made in the field of dementia care. They found that the people they interviewed had plenty to say. They readily acknowledge that their study was with people towards the less severe end of the dementia spectrum, but suggests that Dementia Care Mapping advanced by Kitwood and Bredin (1992) would be another way of obtaining an insight into how the person with dementia experiences the services on offer.

We know that dementia, whatever the type, results in a series of accumulative losses for the affected person, for example, losing the ability to carry out everyday tasks such as dressing and toiletting. There is the loss of short-term and eventually long-term memory. There can be personality change. In the early stages of the disease the person may retain more independence than insight (O'Connor and Kingsley 1994), making service provision difficult. As the illness progresses and with the consequent exaggerated responses to stresses in the environment, people with dementia can display behavioural difficulties such as wandering, agitation, aggression and general disinhibition. They need individualised care from staff with training specific to dementia care.

The accumulative losses of dementia cause an assault on a person's self-confidence. The saying 'Use it or lose it' is very applicable here. If a person with dementia is not allowed, for whatever reason, to continue doing as much for themselves as possible, then they quickly become de-skilled. There are few books which are written by people with dementia because of the inherent difficulties, but Robert Davis's book (1989) is one. He highlights the constant fear of failure, the losses involved as the disease progresses and what this feels like. Charmaz (1983) describes the loss of self which is the most fundamental form of suffering in people with chronic illness and none more so than in those with dementia. So how do they fare when admitted for respite?

Goldberg and Connelly (1982) suggest that a key question in any evaluative research is 'Are the recipients of the service better off for having received it?' In addressing this question, there is a need to explore the impact of respite on the person with dementia and the implications for them of using institutional respite care (Netten 1993).

In one study (Levin *et al.* 1989), the most widely held view amongst carers was that respite had not made much difference to the person with dementia, but it had helped the carer. A few said their relatives were worse off after a period of respite, for example, many become incontinent. A quarter of those admitted benefited in terms of illness being diagnosed or drugs reviewed. Those living alone had company and good food. Seltzer *et al.* (1988) argued that any detrimental effects for mentally frail people are apparent in loss of physical abilities, but even these are not significant. Studies point to respite having a less detrimental effect on the person when in the later stages of the disease.

Any difficulties around disorientation following discharge are short lived (Murphy 1986).

Looking at the impact of the disease on the person with dementia it can be assumed that, like most people going into a new setting, there is a need for adjustment. Because of the impairment suffered, people with dementia have a much more difficult time making these adjustments. The beneficial environment described and advocated by Fleming (1992) is seldom available in respite settings. He suggests an environment should include special characteristics such as important stimuli being highlighted, for example, using colour to make the toilet door obvious, reducing extraneous stimulation, for example, not having the television on all the time, and having total visual access to help orientate the cognitively impaired person and reduce stress. Netten (1993) also emphasises the need for quiet. These are very important considerations given that, on being admitted to respite care, an individual often has to fit into what must seem a confusing and highly stressful environment. People with dementia need a routine, but it is their own routine which is needed, not that of the institution.

Although the number of places available is decreasing, many people are offered respite care in continuing care wards. Patterns of care in these settings are often unsuitable. It has been well documented (Norton *et al.* 1962, Horrocks 1988, Clark and Bowling 1989) that nursing care is frequently task-orientated. Physical care is often unsatisfactory, but the aspects of care which contribute to self-esteem and maintaining a sense of self, such as choice and attention to individual need, may well be missing. Often interaction occurs only when physical tasks such as bathing and toiletting are carried out (Nolan and Grant 1992). Benefits arising from assessment, for example, changes to medication, treatment of infections and, in some cases, rehabilitation of the person during a respite admission, have been noted (Bermann and Foster 1978). There is, however, little information about the person's routine, the individual usually having to conform to that of the institution.

In local authority residential homes, Allen (1983) found that respite users were acceptable to staff if reasonably self-sufficient, but were perceived as problematic once they became dependent or confused. Staff appeared to have only a limited knowledge of the needs of the respite users and there was little or no attempt to individualise care.

The paid carer

Staff working in institutional respite facilities, whether social work or health, have an impact not only on the person with dementia, but also their carers. If the latter are to avail themselves of respite, it is important to look at the staff group and its effect.

Berman *et al.* (1987) noted that the introduction of respite beds into a long-term facility resulted in an improvement of staff morale. Allen (1983) found that staff viewed people coming in for respite care as often being disruptive to other clients. Others have noted that there was a general failure of staff to see beyond the provision of a break (Twigg 1989, Brody 1981) and little was done to address the wider needs of carers. The lack of information during respite was one of the main complaints. Staff appeared to be largely unaware of the guilt carers experience (Twigg 1989, Tyler 1989). In one study, staff had little patience with carers who complained about the service (Boldy and Kuh 1984).

However, in mitigation, staff often have little training to look after people with dementia. One study has shown that training reduced the sickness levels in staff (Lardner and Nicholson 1990) and for that alone had been a sound investment. Training offers staff an opportunity to increase their knowledge base of dementia, improves their management of difficult behaviours and thus promotes confidence and job satisfaction. Training is a resource issue.

Ehrlich and White (1991) detail the clinically based training programme that staff have found useful in domiciliary respite. They use an expanded version of the Global Deterioration Scale which links appropriate respite service interventions to present carer and client characteristics. One beneficial outcome of this model, according to Ehrlich and White, is staff who are 'not only technically competent but also who understand the principles upon which their interventions are based' (p.689).

Some studies have shown people who are offered and accept respite tend to be in the later stages of dementia and consequently need a great deal of care. Staffing levels in many local authority homes have remained similar to those ten years ago when people using the service were able to do many more things for themselves. Looking at respite in a wider context, the whole situation is in a state of flux. Long-stay wards are closing down, staff being redeployed or worse. The trend in social work and health is for departments to be purchasers rather than providers of care. These changes will inevitably have an impact on services.

Innovative services

If such factors as flexibility, usefulness, accessibility, quality and involvement of carers and people with dementia (whatever their age or ethnic origin) are highlighted as important criteria for judging a quality respite service, then which services have these characteristics? What are service examples which make respite care a positive experience for both the carer and the person with dementia?

The recent respite provision in Stratheden Hospital in Fife and the domus units in Stranraer, Dumfries and Galloway (Thomas 1995) demonstrate that quality respite care for people with dementia can be achieved within the health service. Both are small, domestic in size and concentrate on fitting in with the person's routine, making the break a positive and stimulating experience for the person, and an acceptable, beneficial one for the carer. For some carers, hospital respite, with the emphasis on assessment, can be more acceptable than the more social type of respite break. It is also free of charge.

Rosebank, a local authority residential home in Kilmarnock, Strathclyde, which includes a dementia unit, offers many of the above characteristics (Archibald 1991). Without a massive increase in resources, it has been innovative in listening to and responding to the needs of both the carer and the person with dementia. The individual is offered daycare in a small homely setting with plenty of cues to help orientation. Carers can take advantage of the transport for mainstream daycare or choose to bring their relative in themselves. The latter takes away the stress of having to be ready in time for the van arriving and also has the advantage of providing an opportunity to meet and talk to staff on a regular basis. Staff compile life-story books so they get to know the person in some depth. Residential respite is within the same unit as daycare so it is a relatively painless transition. Each person has a single room and an effort is made to find out about his/her routine. There is a wide range of activities. Carers can use daycare and residential respite as flexibly as they need. Immediate respite is provided for a few hours if the carer feels very stressed. They can also bring their relative in to the unit overnight if things are proving too much. The home also provides a 24-hour telephone help line for carers. On one occasion the help line was used regularly by a person with dementia who was disorientated. Phoning the home meant they were not phoning their carer at all times of the day and night. Staff have had and continue to have training. They have developed expertise in managing challenging behaviours so that medications have been reduced.

What can be achieved when health and social services work together is demonstrated by an innovative scheme in Cambridgeshire (Seaborn 1992). The service that emerged was a respite bed for people with dementia in a local authority home controlled by carers. This has allowed flexibility and an offshoot has been the social support gleaned by carers in the group scheme. A community psychiatric nurse instigated the project and, since the bed has been available, nobody involved has been admitted to a psychiatric hospital for emergency respite care.

Family-based respite care is offered by the Share Project in Strathclyde, a recent service development. Prospective individuals and/or families are recruited to offer short periods of respite to people with dementia in a family setting. Alternatively, the person with dementia remains in his or her own home and the recruited individual will stay with the person for an identified respite period. This is really useful when a person lives alone and moving them out of their home might have a disorientating effect and jeopardise their return home.

Alzheimer's Scotland – Action on Dementia (ASAD) has addressed the issue of flexible innovative respite and reduced considerably the feelings of guilt among relatives by referring to the respite as a holiday together for both carer and cared for. ASAD provides respite care where a group of carers accompanied by their relative with dementia, plus a group of volunteers, rents a house or caravan for a week. The volunteers provide support and back up, act as sitters for carers and, importantly, cook the meals. The last of these seems to be a very important consideration. Most of those who avail themselves of the service are spouses. If the findings of Levin *et al.*'s study (1989), where older spouses were the least likely to accept respite care, is representative, then this model might be a way of making the service more acceptable to them. It is certainly a factor in reducing feelings of guilt and is helpful when carers cannot or will not let go of their caring role, albeit for a short time.

In Central Region interesting and innovative services have been created. One example is daycare provided by local people who have

an 'open home' once a week. Volunteers are recruited and paid gener-
ous expenses. Holiday breaks and long-term 'fostering' have also been
a feature (Mitchell 1993).

Some dementia projects in Scotland deploy sessional workers for
overnight stays, but financial constraints again limit the service on
offer. ASAD's Edinburgh branch offers home respite, allocating a maximum of 24 hours to each person who applies. This can be for two nights,
for 'one-off' situations or it can be a 'holding' operation until statutory
services take over.

In Melbourne, Australia, a daycare service housed in a bungalow
has folding beds which are used to provide overnight care in a place
which is familiar to the person (Archibald 1992). It concentrates on
trying to offer respite care which fulfils the needs of both the carer and
the person with dementia. This is not always achieved in many services.

The Govan Dementia Project Glasgow (Illsley 1992), providing
daycare from a council flat, also offers a night monitoring service. All
its clients live alone and this service, by calling in at least twice a night
to put the person to bed or simply to make sure he or she is at home
and not wandering, helps reduce anxiety and stress in carers who live
some distance away.

What is apparent with all these innovative schemes is that they give
a sense of control and choice to the carer involved. Within the financial
constraints imposed, they offer a flexible service which is one of the
hallmarks of quality. They also help in supporting people with dementia for longer and thus, arguably, delaying long-term care.

But does respite care delay long-term care?

Respite care is often advocated as a means of preventing long-term
care. However, in a number of studies this assumption is questioned
(Levin *et al.* 1989, Gilhooley 1986, Brodaty and Gresham 1992). In his
study, Melzer (1990) reports that, on existing evidence, the planner's
assumption of a preventative effect of respite care, in avoiding admission to institutional care, is unjustified. Research highlights the different functions that short-term care has for different people. There is
evidence to suggest that the availability of respite can encourage
reluctant carers to either take on or continue caring. Some studies point
to an increased likelihood that those using respite would consider

long-term care in the coming years (Levin *et al.* 1989, 1993). George (1986) reports that the carers who showed the highest level of service use were those who then decided to seek long-term care for their relative. She suggests two reasons: either carers do not accept or seek services until late in the caregiving process, or else they have already decided on long-term care and are simply using respite services until that can be achieved.

Some studies show that regular respite was a precursor to long-term care. Levin *et al.* (1989) describe how those people receiving regular respite care at the initial interview were far more likely to be in permanent residential care on follow up than those with occasional relief admissions or those who had never had respite. Possible reasons for this are given in two studies (Allen 1983, Levin *et al.* 1989), with several factors highlighted. One is that when carers were in receipt of respite care, professionals were more understanding of what the former had to contend with. Second, respite care was used as preparation for long-term care for all concerned. The person became accustomed to the place and staff, as did the carer. The heads of residential homes often viewed respite as a trial admission period. Third, some carers, when provided with an opportunity to get off what they saw as the treadmill of caring, wanted permanent 'respite'. Fourth, respite was used as a means of delaying rather than preventing long-term care. It was a means of supporting a family until a long term-bed became available.

Gilhooley (1986) found that, while carers valued services and admitted they could not have coped without them, they would still have preferred long-term care for their relative. Carers have different needs and strengths. Askham and Thomson (1990) found that in terms of either delaying or preventing long-term admission, it was the carer's desire to go on caring which was the most significant factor. Other studies support this finding.

Conclusion

In this chapter, issues have been raised which question certain assumptions commonly held by people working in health and social care settings. The view that respite care is crucial to enable carers to go on caring is only partly true. While very important in enabling some people to continue to care, for a substantial group respite care is often not available until the late stages, is unsuitable to their or their relative's needs, and often is inflexible. It is all too frequently seen simply as a break, with the potential for support, information sharing and education being missed. Respite does enable some carers to continue caring, but at a price, in terms of guilt, in terms of effects on their health, in terms of keeping an untenable situation going until such time as a 'permanent' bed becomes available. Rather than preventing, respite seems to be more about rationing and delaying long-term admission.

Used in a constructive way, respite care can be a positive experience. Caring for someone with dementia has a number of positive aspects which are often forgotten or not even considered. Knowing that a range of respite care is available at an early stage in the illness, at times when input is needed, which is affordable and which, importantly, ties in with the needs of the person with dementia, can contribute to carers' well-being and help them to cope.

Respite care can allow a gradual 'letting go' to occur so that both carer and the person with dementia are more prepared for the eventual long-term admission. Respite can provide assessment and rehabilitation to improve quality of life for both parties. When staff see carers as co-workers, and respect and use the carer's knowledge of the person with dementia, respite care can become more acceptable and less stressful to all concerned. When asked, carers generally report that they benefit from respite. However, if Lindsay *et al.*'s (1993) analogy of a patchwork quilt is used, it would seem that at present, with regard to respite care, whether domiciliary or residential, carers, the person with dementia and service providers are obliged to 'make do and mend'. Overall, the findings of research support the conclusion that respite care promotes the capacity of the carer to go on caring, whether they want to or not.

References

Allen, I. (1983) *Short Stay Residential Care for the Elderly*. London: Policy Studies Institute.

Alzheimer's Disease Society (1992) Alzheimer's Disease Report England. London: Alzheimer's Disease Society.

Archibald, C. (1991) *Rosebank*. Stirling: Dementia Services Development Centre.

Archibald, C. (1992) *The Australian Experience*. Stirling: Dementia Services Development Centre.

Askham, J. and Thomson, C. (1990) *Dementia and Home Care*, Research Paper 4. London: Age Concern, Institute of Gerontology.

Badger, F. and Cameron, E. (1990) 'Waiting to be served.' *Health Service Journal 100*, 11 January, 54–55.

Berman, S., Delaney, N., Gallagher, D., Atins, P. and Graeber, M.P. (1987) 'Respite care: a partnership between a veterans' administration nursing home and families to care for frail elders at home.' *Gerontologist 27*, 5, 581–584.

Bermann, K. and Foster, E.M. (1978) 'Management of the demented elderly patient in the community.' *British Journal of Psychiatry 132*, 441–449.

Berry, G., Zarit, S. and Rabatin, V. (1991) 'Care giver activity on respite and non respite days: a comparison of two services approaches.' *Gerontologist 32*, 6, 830–835.

Boldy, D. and Kuh, D. (1984) 'Short-term care for the elderly in residential homes: a research note.' *British Journal of Social Work 14*, 2, April, 173–174.

Bowers, B.J. (1987) 'Intergenerational caregiving: adult caregivers and their ageing parents.' In M. Nolan and G. Grant (eds) *Regular Respite*, Research Paper 6. London: Age Concern Institute of Gerontology.

Broadaty, H. and Gresham, M. (1992) 'Prescribing residential respite care for dementia – effects, side effects, indications and dosage.' *International Journal of Geriatric Psychiatry 7*, 357–362.

Brody, E. (1981) 'Women in the middle and family help to older people.' *The Gerontologist 21*, 471–481.

Brook, P. and Jestice, S. (1986) 'Relief for the demented and their carers.' *Geriatric Medicine*, June, 31–36.

Charmaz, K. (1983) 'Loss of self: A fundamental form of suffering in the chronically ill.' *Sociology of Health and Illness*, 168–195.

Clark, P. and Bowling, A. (1989) 'An observational study of quality of life in NHS nursing homes and a long-stay hospital ward for the elderly.' *Ageing and Society 9*, 3–13.

Corcoran, M. (1992) 'Gender differences in dementia management plans of spousal caregivers: Implications for occupational therapy.' *American Journal of Occupational Therapy 46*, November, 11.

Cox, M.S. and McClennan, M.J. (1994) *A Guide to Early Onset Dementia*. Stirling: Dementia Services Development Centre.

Crossman, L., London, C. and Barry, C. (1981) 'Older women caring for disabled spouses: a model for supportive services.' *The Gerontologist 21*, 464–470.

Davis, R. (1989) *My Journey into Alzheimer's Disease*. Illinois: Tyndale Marie Publishers.

Eagles, M. and Gilleard, C.J. (1984) 'The functions and effectiveness of a day hospital for the dementing elderly.' Edinburgh: *Health Bulletins 42*, 87–91.

Ehrlich, P. and White, J. (1991) 'TOPS: A consumer approach to Alzheimer's respite programs.' *The Gerontologist 32*, 5, 686–691.

Equal Opportunities Commission (1980) *The Experience of Caring for Elderly and Handicapped Dependents*. London: Equal Opportunities Commission.

Fleming, R. (1992) *Issues of Assessment and Design for Longstay Care*. Stirling: Dementia Services Development Centre.

George, L. (1986) 'Respite care: evaluating a strategy for Easing Caregiver Burden Center.' *Advances in Research 10*, 2, 1–10.

Gilhooley, M.L.M. (1986) 'Senile dementia: factors associated with care-givers' preference for institutional care.' *British Journal of Medical Psychology 59*, 165–171.

Goldberg, E.M. and Connelly, N. (1982) *The Effectiveness of Social Care for the Elderly: An Overview of Recent and Current Evaluative Research*. London: Heinemann Educational Books.

Haley, W. and Pardo, K. (1989) 'Relationships of severity of dementia to caregiving stressors.' *Psychology and Ageing 4*, 389–392.

Hedley, R. (1991) *Not Enough Care*. London: Alzheimer Disease Society.

Heptinstall, D. (1989) 'Black and white choice for elderly consumers.' *Social Work Today*, August, 12–13.

Hochschild, A. (1989) *The Second Shift: Working Parents and the Revolution at Home*. New York: Viking Penguin.

Homer, A. and Gilleard, C. (1994) 'The effect of in-patient respite care on elderly patients and their carers.' *Age and Ageing 23*, 274–276.

Horrocks, P. (1988) 'Caring in hospital.' In S. Tomlin (ed) *Abuse of Elderly: An Unnecessary and Preventable Problem*. London: British Geriatric Society.

Horrowitz, A. (1985) 'Sons and daughters as caregivers to older parents: differences in role performance and consequences.' *The Gerontologist 25*, 612–617.

Illsley, J. (1992) *Govan Dementia Project Day and Night Care*. Stirling: Dementia Services Development Centre.

Jacques, A. (1994) *Health Board Survey*. Stirling: Dementia Services Development Centre.

Jones, D.A. and Peters, T.J. (1992) 'Caring for elderly dependants: effects on the carers' quality of life.' *Age and Ageing 21*, 421–428.

Kitwood, T. and Bredin, K. (1992) 'A new approach to the evaluation of dementia care.' *Journal of Advances in Health and Nursing Care 1*, 5, 41–60.

Kosloski, K. and Montgomery, R. (1993) 'Perceptions of respite services as predictors of utilisation.' *Research on Ageing 15*, 4, December, 399–413.

Lardner, R. and Nicholson, E. (1990) *Nurse In-service Training in a Psychogeriatric Unit.* Stirling: Dementia Services Development Centres.

Lawton, M.P., Brody, E. and Saperstein, A. (1989) 'A controlled study of respite service for caregivers of Alzheimer's patients.' *The Gerontologist* 29, 1, 8–16.

Levin, E., Moriarty, J. and Gorbach, P. (1993) *The Value of Respite Care.* London: National Institute for Social Work.

Levin, E., Moriarty, J. and Gorbach, P. (1994) *Better for the Break.* London: HMSO.

Levin, E., Sinclair, I. and Gorbach, P. (1989) *Families, Services and Confusion in Old Age.* Aldershot: Gower.

Lindow, V. and Morris, J. (1994) *Service User Involvement: Synthesis of Findings and Experience in the Field of Community Care.* First draft report to the Joseph Rowntree Foundation.

Lindsay, M., Kohl, M. and Collins, J. (1993) *The Patchwork Quilt: A Study of Respite Care Services in Scotland.* Edinburgh: Social Work Services Inspectorate for Scotland.

Maxwell, R.J. (1984) 'Quality assessment in health.' *British Medical Journal* 288, 1470–1471.

Melzer, D. (1990) 'An evaluation of a respite care unit for elderly people with dementia: a framework and some results.' *Health Trends 22*, 2.

Mitchell, R. (1993) *Going Fishing.* Annual Report Central Regional Council, Social Work Unit, Bellsdyke Hospital.

Murphy, E. (1986) *Dementia and Mental Illness in the Old.* London: Macmillan.

Netten, A. (1993) *A Positive Environment?* Aldershot: Ashgate.

Nolan, M. and Grant, G. (1992) *Regular Respite. An Evaluation of a Hospital Rota Bed Scheme for Elderly People.* London: Age Concern Institute of Gerontology Research Paper, 6.

Norton, D., McClaren, R. and Exton-Smith, A.N. (1962) *An Investigation of Geriatric Nursing Problems in Hospital: Research Report NCCOP.* Edinburgh: Churchill Livingstone.

O'Connor, P. and Kingsley, E. (1994) *When All Else Fails.* Paper available from Curtin University School of Nursing, Perth, Western Australia.

Parker, G. (1985) *With Due Care and Attention: A Review of Research on Informal Care.* London: Family Policy Studies Centre.

Pearson, N. (1988) 'An assessment of relief hospital admissions for elderly patients with dementia.' *Health Trends 20*, 120–121.

Poonia, K. and Ward, L. (1990) 'Fair share of (the) care?' *Community Care 798*, 16–18.

Pruchno, R.A. and Resch, N.L. (1989) 'Husbands and wives as caregivers: antecedents of depression and burden.' *The Gerontologist 29*, 159–165.

Qureshi, H. and Walker, A. (1989) *The Caring Relationship*. London: Macmillan.

Seaborn, A. (1992) 'Making a break.' *Nursing Times 88*, October 14, 44–52.

Seltzer, B., Rheaume, Y., Volicer, L., Fabiszewski, K.J., Lyon, P.C., Brown, J.E. and Volicer, B. (1988) 'The short-term effects of in-hospital respite on the patient with Alzheimer's disease.' *The Gerontologist 28*, 1, 121–124.

Sheldon, F. (1982) 'Supporting the supporters: working with the relatives of patients with dementia.' *Age and Ageing 11*, 184–188.

Social Services Inspectorate (1993) *Inspecting for Quality*. London: HMSO.

Sperlinger, D. and McAuslane, L. (1994) 'I don't want you to think I'm ungrateful... but it doesn't satisfy what I want.' A pilot study of the views of users of services for people with dementia in the London Borough of Sutton. Dept of Psychology, St Heliers Trust Sutton Hospital, Cotswold Road, Sutton, Surrey.

Thomas, M. (1995) *Innistaigh: A Domus Unit in Stranraer*. Stirling: Dementia Services Development Centre.

Twigg, J. (1989) *Evaluating Services in Support of Informal Carers in SPRU and Informal Care*. Social Policy Research Unit, University of York.

Twigg, J. (1992) *Carers: Research and Practice*. London: HMSO.

Tyler, J. (1989) *Respite Care for the Elderly*. Unpublished M.Phil. thesis, Cranfield Institute of Technology.

Webb, I. (1987) *People Who Care: A Report on Carer Provision in England and Wales*. London: Cooperative Women's Guild.

Zarit, S., Todd, P.A. and Zarit, J.M. (1986) 'Subjective burden of husbands and wives as caregivers: a longitudinal study.' *The Gerontologist 26*, 260–266.

Chapter 9

Cairdeas House

Developing Good Practice in Short Breaks for Individuals with Mental Health Problems

Alison Petch

'Respite is almost wholly absent as a concept within the mental health sector.' (Twigg and Atkin 1994, p.116)

Introduction

The provision of short-term care is at a premium throughout the UK. The situation in Scotland has recently been reported as resembling a 'patchwork quilt' (Lindsay *et al.* 1993). For individuals with mental health problems (excluding dementia), the number of patches offered is very few indeed – a 'dearth in all directions' (p.17). Researchers were only able to identify clearly four community-based services, and only one of these, to be presented below, was a dedicated service. The number of beds was estimated as 40, giving a total annual figure of 1800 weeks (85% occupancy) or 2.2 per cent of the total across all care groups. It was calculated in addition that perhaps 988 weeks would be accessed as hospital beds. Various forms of domiciliary support, in particular befriending and sitting services, may also offer a break, either to a carer or to the individual with mental health problems.

Much of the debate around the concept (and terminology) of short-term care has to be examined anew in relation to individuals with mental health problems. Traditionally there tends to be some notion of a break from a primary carer, with differing emphasis as to the prime beneficiary. Much has been made of the need for carers to get a break; more recently there has been a greater concern that the period should be enjoyable for the individual in need of support. There should be the opportunity for self-determination, for an individual to express his or her desire or need for 'time out' or for a holiday.

Experience to date, however, tends to derive from the care of older people and of individuals, particularly children, with learning disabilities. Apart from admission to beds in psychiatric hospitals, there have not been the facilities to document the experiences of individuals with mental health problems. It is not surprising, then, that very little research has been carried out in this field. It can be argued, however, that there are factors particular to the mental health field which may distinguish provision in this area. In particular, the number of individuals with immediate carers is likely to be lower (and therefore 'respite' may indeed be an inappropriate term). Furthermore, where carers are present, the nature of their caring role is likely to be different – possibly fewer physical tasks, but much emotional support and sustaining, and what Twigg and Atkin (1994) have characterised as 'being responsible'. Individual needs may fluctuate and there may be less predictability to the caring role. Most importantly, individuals with mental health problems are less likely to be placed in short-term care against their volition.

As for any other group, the need for short-term care or a break can be met by a variety of responses. The individual with mental health problems could spend time in an alternative residential setting, support could be provided on a domiciliary basis, or the individual could move to some other family care setting. Traditional use of hospital-based care, often not for 'medical' reasons but in response to the needs of the carer, has depended upon the discretion of individuals and is increasingly unlikely as the number of psychiatric beds continues to decline.

A distinction must also be made between crisis care and short-term care, although at the margins there may be overlap. Indeed the recognition that individuals with mental health problems may at times express a desire for sanctuary, for retreat or for asylum, a wish that may occur irrespective of the living situation, suggests an interpretation of the concept very particular to this group.

As prefaced above, there is as yet only one dedicated facility for individuals with mental health problems in Scotland, and it is believed to be the only model of its kind in Britain. In 1992, Penumbra Respite Care established Cairdeas House, a guest house offering stays of up to three weeks. 'Cairdeas' is a gaelic word meaning 'fellowship, respite and harmony'. It was the first provision of its type and addressed a perceived need for planned breaks, both for carers and users. It is used by people from all over Scotland, and some from south of the border. This chapter will explore the user perspective on this particular model of short-term care.

Cairdeas House

Although individual befriending arrangements may have existed, it is often only with the establishment of a physical facility that a landmark is created. There was considerable planning and preparation in the months prior to Cairdeas House taking its first guests. A project manager and volunteer manager were appointed in January 1992 as the upgrading of the property in central Edinburgh was nearing completion. A grant was secured from the Unemployed Voluntary Action Fund for the volunteer manager's post and for volunteer expenses. Renovation of a Victorian property to a high standard was to produce guest accommodation for a maximum of 13 individuals in eight rooms, with office accommodation in the basement. Considerable effort and money was expended in creating an attractive environment, indicative of the philosophy of valuing the individual. Although the project was registered for a maximum of 13, the eight rooms are only shared by choice and this rarely happens, a major consideration in financial terms. Individual items of furniture were bought at auction and the natural features of the house enhanced. There is a television and telephone in every room.

Initially, it was proposed that additional support to guests, beyond that available from the two core staff, should be offered through a network of volunteers and the first volunteers were recruited and trained. The aspiration of Cairdeas House was to provide planned breaks for individuals with mental health problems and/or their carers in an atmosphere of support and relaxation (Penumbra Discussion Paper on Respite Care 1989). The model was to be the booked 'holiday' rather than responding to the unanticipated crisis. The philosophy of care underlying Cairdeas House centres on a valuing of individual experience and choice, emphasising the right of guests to spend their time as they wish. The project also aims to raise people's self-esteem by offering them a 'break' within exceptionally pleasant, indeed elegant, surroundings.

The first guests at Cairdeas House stayed in the summer of 1992. Two factors emerged at this stage which led to radical rethinking of the basis of the project. First, the level of support available through the volunteer structure could in no way meet the requirements of a project that needed cover for 24 hours, seven days a week. In particular, stability and continuity were inevitably absent. Second, the regional council had concluded that the project required registration through the social work department and this process was initiated.

Cairdeas House opened in its present form in November 1992, staffed by an additional five project workers (two of whom were initial volunteers), plus the cook/housekeeper. Sleep-over duties were formalised. Under the new arrangements the cost of a seven-day stay rose from £260 to £325 and latterly £345. Volunteers (approximately 15) continued to play an important role, but one less concerned with the ongoing running of the guest house and more with befriending and leisure activities, both within the house and more widely in Edinburgh and beyond. Staff members were selected on the basis of their ability, *inter alia*, to appreciate the individuality of each guest and to enhance their empowerment. The characteristic of 'a big chunk of genuineness' was cited.

Placement

Major variation among Scottish regions in the practice of assessment prior to a short-term placement has had very significant implications for the development of Cairdeas House. The policies adopted reflect, as prefaced above, very different ideologies as to the nature and purpose of short-term care. One region, Central, having allocated monies under the mental illness specific grant (MISG), adopted a low-key approach to assessing need for a short-term break. One of two designated officers visited the individual to discuss his or her requirements. Approval for a visit, and the corresponding finance, lay within their remit. Central had, in fact, been considering a provision of its own and decided instead to seek MISG funding with which they could 'spot purchase' places from Penumbra. Tayside adopted a similar model, purchasing 30 places in the project over a 12-month period.

Elsewhere, however, most noticeably Lothian, any request for a break at Cairdeas House precipitated a full assessment of need, together with a financial assessment of means. The requirement for the financial decision means that, even if the individual has been deemed in need of a break, a place is not necessarily allocated.

Two important issues would appear to be at stake. First, a definition of respite which requires that a need be proven through assessment suggests a crisis rather than preventive model. Is it not equally valid to define a respite break as one that enhances quality of life and improves well-being on the terms to which any individual might aspire? The requirement, to be deemed 'in need' denies the individual's right to exercise choice, and to make direct application themselves for a facility from which they believe they will benefit. Second, the rigid assessment model raises the inevitable question of 'whose needs?': how, for example, are the relative needs of the individual with mental health problems and the carer to be prioritised?

Guest response

From a very early stage it was considered important to gather the responses of those who stayed at Cairdeas House. With such a new and untested facility there was a concern to ensure that both the physical provision and the support structure were being favourably received.

The author was asked to devise a questionnaire, to be completed by guests at the end of their stay. Completion of the questionnaire was built into the final day's routine and staff were available to lend assistance if required. Although several pages long, and at first sight possibly somewhat daunting, virtually all the questions were of a 'tick box' format. Simple demographic data was collected at the end of the questionnaire and the opportunity offered for individuals to add 'anything else that you would like to say about Cairdeas House and your visit here'. Questionnaires in a not dissimilar format were also devised for carers and volunteers; the project only made use of these, however, with a small number of carers.

By July 1993 a total of 87 questionnaires had been completed by individuals who had stayed at Cairdeas House. A total of 130 guests stayed during the period between November 1992 and July 1993, suggesting a completion rate of two-thirds. The majority of guests (66) had spent a week at the facility. Five individuals had spent less than a week and 15 more. (One respondent did not record the duration of their visit.) Almost two-thirds of the guests (53) normally lived in Central Region, a product of the funding arrangements discussed above. A further four visited from Penumbra's house in the Western Isles. Three individuals came from south of the border, the others, from Strathclyde, Lothian and Fife.

Male guests (52) outnumbered female (34) – with one not recording their gender. Individuals came from a range of living situations. Thirty-four normally lived on their own, 24 with family members and 4 with non-relatives. Nineteen came from supported accommodation, one from a hostel and two from a hospital base. (Three guests omitted to provide this information.)

A large majority of the guests had been in contact with mental health services over a lengthy period. All but 22 had at least five years contact, while 43 had ten years or more. At the upper end were 13 individuals in contact with services for 25 years or more. (Information was missing for eight individuals.)

Application

Cairdeas House had devoted some energy to publicising its existence, including approaches to social work authorities, use of the media and advertisements in the professional journals. Inevitably, however, the funding considerations outlined above had influenced the sources of successful applicants. Fifty-four reported that their visit had been funded by a social work department, six by a health board and seven through a charitable organisation. Two reported that Penumbra itself had funded the visit, one cited a lawyer and one a London Borough. Four were entirely self-funded, and for a further four, funds were a mix of self and the social work department. Eight did not supply this information.

Individuals had heard of Cairdeas House from a variety of sources. Predominant were either statutory or voluntary sector workers, with 22 citing a social worker, six a community nurse and 16 a support or project worker. Seventeen mentioned their local mental health association as the source of information, an influence of the promotion of the facility in Central Region. Other sources of information included a hospital development worker (five), the NSF newsletter (two), and, in one case, a psychiatrist.

For the majority, a professional worker submitted the application to Cairdeas House on their behalf, frequently a social worker. Nine people applied directly themselves and two had a carer make the application on their behalf. Only a minority (25) had specified a particular date in their application; all but five had been given the period they had requested. Lack of flexibility in booking arrangements is a common problem in many other residential short-term care facilities.

The variety of reasons for which individuals came to Cairdeas House are summarised below. Additionally, one said they had come 'to think in a different environment'. This comment is worthy of note, the project being on offer as a 'bridge to new circumstances', for example, a period of reflection for someone in supported accommodation contemplating change. The holiday element is predominant, a feature for four out of five. Specific reference to giving a carer a break is made by only 15; it must be remembered, however, that only 24 were living with family members and a further four with non-relatives.

Table 9.1. Reasons for staying at Cairdeas House

n = 85	no. citing	% of reasons
to have a holiday	70	43.0
to have some support	24	14.7
to meet other people	23	14.1
for a change of scene	16	9.8
to give a carer a break	15	9.2
to visit Edinburgh	15	9.2
	163	100.0

All but 15 felt they had sufficient information about Cairdeas House before they arrived. Those who elaborated on what else they would have liked to have known referred to what the place looked like, some information about Edinburgh, what they should bring. One spoke of 'being assured it's really for us... we could not understand how it looked in photographs and how it was meant for us', reflecting both a low level of expectation and the unusually high standard of accommodation on offer.

Nineteen people said they had worries before coming to Cairdeas House. These ranged over both the practical and the emotional: anxieties about meeting other people and fitting in, about being alone and away from home, about having enough money, about 'the routine and if it would be like hospital'. Prospective guests were encouraged to make an initial visit to inform themselves about the project, but for many this was not possible.

Asked to choose the statement that best summarised their feelings before coming to Cairdeas House, the guests responded as shown in Table 9.2.

Table 9.2. Statements summarising guests' feelings before arrival

n = 85	*no. citing*	*% of statements*
'delighted at the prospect of a break from routine'	63	75.0
'worried about exactly what it would be like'	16	19.0
'not really bothered – for someone else's convenience, not mine'	5	6.0
	84	100.0

For some, a certain amount of anxiety is inevitable; one can only speculate as to whether the balance could be shifted more towards the first category.

In practical terms, the majority of guests arrived at Cairdeas House in the company of others. Thirty-four were in group visits involving a number from the same area, while 31 were accompanied on the journey by a carer, friend or volunteer. Only 20, therefore, came on their own. Five people cited problems in getting to Cairdeas House, three because they were unfamiliar with the area, one due to agoraphobia and one because the individual had 'no motivation due to exhaustion'.

While in Cairdeas House, the information available to project staff on individual guests derives from the initial referral information, plus in the case, for example, of Lothian, the assessment form and care plan. This information is not shared with volunteers. A handover book is maintained day to day, with open access to all guests.

Accommodation

Individuals were asked a number of detailed questions about the accommodation on offer at Cairdeas House. Responses were in the main very favourable, 68 rating it 'very comfortable'.

Similar levels of satisfaction were expressed with the rest of the house. Eighty-three selected 'homely and comfortable' as the most apt description, only one opting for 'too big and overwhelming'. Asked to select the best feature of the house, comments ranged from the style of furnishings and decorations, and the warmth, to the 'pictures and lights', 'bathroom very close and just right', 'lots of room, lovely facilities, well sited'.

In selecting the worst feature of the house many drew a blank. One referred to 'the kitchen being locked so no midnight snacks'. Given the nature of the building, disabled access is a problem at Cairdeas House. Wheelchair access is impossible and the stairs are difficult even for those with only moderate physical disability.

An important feature of any stay, the catering, was well received, a cook being employed to provide all meals. Breakfast is available from 8.30 to 10.00am, there is a light lunch at 1.00pm and everyone sits down to a two-course dinner at 6.00pm.

Activities

The policy of the staff at Cairdeas House is to maximise informality and individuality. Rules and structures are therefore kept to a minimum. Alcohol is not allowed within the house and certain areas are not for smoking. A routine is generated by the meal times, with guests, supported by staff and volunteers, planning a range of activities both in the house and elsewhere during their stay.

Asked how they had spent most of their time at Cairdeas House, seven spoke of being in the house itself, 19 of being out and about in Edinburgh, and 59 a mixture of the two (two missing). The project has the use of a car which can both assist with local transport for the less mobile and be used for trips further afield. The activities pursued outside the house are given in Table 9.3, a total of 299 events being recorded by the 84 who completed this question.

'Other' included two who mentioned a trip to Fife, one who went out with his girlfriend and one who went to the hairdressers, illustrating the 'ordinary' nature of activities for some, as opposed to the limited

Table 9.3. Activities pursued outside Cairdeas House

n = 84	no. involved	% of guests
walking around Edinburgh	68	81.0
sightseeing in Edinburgh	66	78.6
shopping	50	60.0
going to cafes	42	50.0
visiting theatre/cinema	31	36.9
sports activities	15	17.9
galleries/museums/zoo, etc.	14	16.6
visiting the pub	5	6.0
other	8	9.5

opportunities available to people receiving short-term care in hospital settings.

Asked about activities within the house, guests were again given a list of six possibilities and asked to add others they had been involved in. The majority at various times spent their time in the house relaxing, watching television, listening to music and talking to other guests. A minority were involved in arts and crafts activities, in playing various games or in reading. Clear favourites among the house-based activities were, first, taking part in discussions with other guests (cited by 25) and, second, general relaxation (20). Least favourite, by a clear margin, was watching television (21).

Individuals were asked if there were other things they would have liked to have done during their stay at Cairdeas House. A range of suggestions was made, the majority citing places they would have liked to have visited (such as the castle, zoo and botanical gardens) or activities they would have liked to pursue (for example, ten-pin bowling, badminton). One very specific request was the opportunity to 'research the family tree'.

Table 9.4. Activities within Cairdeas House

n = 84	*no. involved*	*% of guests*
watching television	66	78.6
discussion with other guests	64	76.2
relaxation	60	71.4
listening to music	60	71.4
reading	28	33.3
art and craft activities	11	13.1
games or cards	8	9.5
discussion with staff	4	4.8

Other guests

Individuals differed in the extent to which they knew others who were staying at Cairdeas House at the same time as themselves. Thirty-five knew none of their fellow guests, while 21 knew most or all of them. Twenty-two knew one or two and seven about half of them (one missing response). Over two-thirds were well pleased with the company of the other guests; 11, however, did not feel any great affinity.

Table 9.5. Affinity with other guests

n = 85	*no. involved*	*% of guests*
'they were not really my type – I didn't really get on with them very well'	11	13.0
'I really enjoyed their company'	58	68.2
'it didn't bother me either way'	16	18.8
	85	**100.0**

The level of contact with other guests, as shown in Table 9.6, had varied. Approximately half spent some time on their own, some with the other guests, while just over a third mixed with the others most of the time.

Table 9.6. Level of contact with other guests

n = 85	no. involved	% of guests
'I was involved with them most of the time'	31	36.5
'I saw them now and again'	9	10.6
'I was with them some of the time, on my own at other times'	45	52.9
	85	100.0

Volunteers

As outlined above, an important feature of Cairdeas House is the presence of volunteers. Extensive thought has been given to the complementary roles of staff and volunteers, with considerable effort devoted to the appropriate preparation and support for volunteers.

Volunteers are available both for general contact and support within the house and to accompany individuals and groups on more specific activities outside the house. Although the original application form referred to individual befriending, this had to be modified in order to avoid raising undue expectations. Each volunteer commits a minimum of one four-to-five hour shift per week, with no more than one or two volunteers around at any time. Volunteers receive initial training, have a practice handbook and benefit from regular supervision with the volunteer manager and from group meetings. The initial volunteers were selected following an elaborate recruitment drive which included the local volunteer exchange, television and radio spots and local newspapers. Applicants were carefully screened, only one in three being taken on.

Only three individuals said they had had no contact with a volunteer during their stay. The majority (57) referred to contact on most days, smaller groups, 12 in each case, to contact 'about half of the time' or 'just once or twice'. For the majority, however, the contact was with the body of volunteers as a whole; only 13 spoke of being linked to one particular volunteer. Individuals reported a wide range of activities undertaken with the volunteers, most specifically visits to particular sights and venues. Others referred more generally to 'walks, chats, games, trips in the car' or 'arts and crafts'. The majority (63) felt that the level of volunteer contact was about right; 17 would have liked it to be more and only two, less.

Staff

Staffing levels at the time these questionnaires were completed comprised the project and volunteer managers, the five support workers and the cook/housekeeper. Subsequently some administrative support has relieved the pressure on the project and volunteer managers. It tended, especially initially, to be one or other of these individuals who would take on any more complex individual situation that arose. A two-shift system was operating, with one staff member sleeping overnight. Few demands had been made during the sleep-over period.

The majority (72) considered the number of staff to be about right, and there were few complaints as to their friendliness or helpfulness.

Table 9.7. Guests' opinions on levels of staffing

n = 86	*no. involved*	*% of guests*
'they have all been very friendly and helpful'	80	93.0
'some of them have been very friendly and helpful'	6	7.0
'they are not really very friendly or helpful'	–	–
	86	100.0

A wide variety of ways in which staff had helped individuals was cited. These ranged from practical issues within the house – 'washing, meals and tea', 'washing and drying of clothes', to emotional support – 'make us feel welcome, deal with anxiety, help to enjoy meals', 'adjusting to other guests'. Help and advice also extended outside the house – 'support going to the chemist', 'getting around by car', 'paintings and outings', 'ideas about what to do'.

Achieving the appropriate level of support in a facility such as Cairdeas House requires sensitivity. Virtually all considered that the support they had found available was 'about right'. Only one regarded it as too little and three as too much. Perhaps most important, however, and most difficult to legislate for, was the ethos of staff: 'The attitude of the staff is probably the best I have ever experienced, and many nurses and doctors based in hospitals would do well adopting a similar style.'

The project is linked to a general practice which will administer depot medication or replace forgotten prescriptions. Close collaboration between the practice and project staff enabled them on one occasion to avert a potential acute admission. The individual experiencing crisis was monitored hourly through the night and, with the aid of additional medication, the crisis receded.

Overall impressions

For only half of the guests was their stay at Cairdeas House what they expected. For the others, it differed from their expectations, but almost universally in a positive fashion. It was 'better than expected – I enjoyed being pampered', 'the helpers are so friendly', 'it's like living in a small guesthouse', 'the staff couldn't do enough to help you'. Several had thought it was 'going to be like hospital', and expressed their appreciation at the lack of strict rules or medical orientation – 'it's not like hospital or home – it's like one big happy family'. Only one individual commented that they 'felt lonely in a crowd of people, the odd one out'.

Perhaps the strongest vote, however, in favour of Cairdeas House was the number who would recommend others to visit. Apart from five who omitted this response, all but two would make such a recommendation, while all, bar none, would themselves return. There were some particularly poignant responses, such as 'if a place like Cairdeas House had been available when I first needed it, perhaps my marriage would have been saved.'

Carer responses

With the notable exception of Perring, Twigg and Atkin (1990) and of work directed at family interaction (for example, Leff *et al.* 1982), the burgeoning literature on carers has remained silent in relation to mental health users. Although questionnaires had been prepared for both volunteers and carers, the Project had these completed by only five carers, one only partly. (Note from above, however, that only 24 guests lived with relatives.) All but one were mothers caring for sons, the other a daughter whose mother had lived with her and her family for three years. The mothers described themselves as having been carers for 40, 20 and 13 years respectively. All but one had learnt of Cairdeas House through a social worker and the social work department had borne the majority of the cost. One, however, had paid the £50 deposit, while another had provided £40 in pocket money.

A brief overview of this small number of responses suggests high levels of satisfaction with the facility offered by Cairdeas House. All had found the practical arrangements satisfactory and felt they had sufficient information on Cairdeas House before their family member visited. One expressed particular appreciation of the detailed preparation prior to the visit:

'My husband and I both appreciate the time and care taken before the visit to Cairdeas to prepare M for his stay. It was also very helpful for us to visit Cairdeas and talk with staff beforehand. With the knowledge that he would be well cared for in every way, we were able to relax and spend a holiday away from home.'

Two of the carers used the opportunity to go away – 'able to have a holiday, the two of us on our own, the first time for five years'. Although the other three remained at home, two spent their time doing different things.

All five carers admitted to worries about the individual they cared for going to Cairdeas House. These ranged from concern that the individual might become 'more mentally ill' or be lonely, to worries about medication or whether he or she would be able to cope with meeting new people and living in a different environment, possibly for the first time. One detailed her concerns: 'My mother smokes constantly and talks all the time and won't wash regular'. They also, however, anticipated benefits, most commonly that their relative would have a break from routine: 'a change of environment after years of being at home. I was relieved that A would be with people who really care and make allowances.'

All foresaw the benefits to themselves as focusing on the relief from caring duties: 'greatly relieved that I could get a few days respite from the mental and physical stress of looking after someone with this illness day in day out.' Another elaborated further:

> 'To have a break from M's company; to have some much needed privacy in the home; to be on our own and not have to think where and what he is doing all the time; to have a holiday away from home by ourselves.'

All summed up their own attitude as 'really pleased and looking forward to the break.'

Carers were asked to comment on what their relative told them of their stay at Cairdeas House, to judge the extent to which they had enjoyed it and to elaborate on what they thought had been the benefits for themselves and their relatives. Three out of four felt their relative had 'had a really good time and very much enjoyed it', only one that 'he didn't enjoy it very much at all' because of his dislike of being in a strange place. Despite this response, this carer spoke of her son having enjoyed the food, his room and the garden, and the 'pleasant and understanding staff'. Moreover, she believed that the experience of being away from home had been of benefit to the individual, while she herself 'had a great sense of peace and calmness'. This situation exemplifies the balance that so often has to be struck between the needs and preferences of different individuals within the caring relationship.

Others highlighted the benefits to their relative of having met other people and of having had opportunities to participate in a range of activities, 'with people who understood his moods'. Two of the carers also spoke of detecting signs of increased confidence, 'feeling refreshed and more confident about visiting places on her own and happy to know she made new friends.' The downside of course could be the return to normal routine. 'For her to come back home to her boring routines again and misses all the different adults to have really good conversations with.'

For carers themselves, the benefits followed on from their expectations – 'a complete rest from the caring', 'a relaxing time, very peaceful stress-free week which even my children enjoyed more'.

All the carers who responded wished their relative to visit Cairdeas House again. In summarising the positive experience it provided, one carer highlighted the contrast with previous arrangements:

> 'The house was in a good location for the shops and parks for her which she thought was really good as in the past for respite care she was away up at the hospital which she says was boring and a horrible place to stay even for a short time.'

Conclusion

Cairdeas House is a unique provision. As such it has had to negotiate all the pitfalls to which innovation is exposed, with no role model to provide the framework. It has had to do so, moreover, against a background of both internal and external uncertainty. In retrospect it is apparent that the idea of maintaining a sufficiently intensive support service on a volunteer basis was naive. Moreover, despite the relaxed, holiday atmosphere generated in the house, the complexity of the operation should not be underestimated. The project and volunteer managers had to create a reality out of the germ of an idea. Moreover they had to impose a structure in terms of training, budgets, recruitment and marketing at a time when agencies were preoccupied by all the other demands of the community care agenda. Against such a backcloth the success of the project in the eyes of its users, evident throughout their accounts, is to be commended.

Financial considerations are, however, crucial. A private funder underwrote the first year's deficit at Cairdeas House. Much uncertainty is generated by the demands of those regions which insist on the full assessment procedure and, despite the key role of short-term breaks in maintaining individuals within the community, do not cover the full cost. Perversely, those regions which have responded to concerns at the high charges for short-term placements by introducing a flat rate, may have created a disincentive to those for whom even the fixed charge remains problematic, since this is not means-tested. The local authority is not obliged to assess ability to pay for the first eight weeks of short-term care, although it can, if it wishes, charge a 'reasonable rate', but after that is obliged to charge residents at the standard rate and to means-test (Scottish Office 1992). Far more satisfactory was the low-key screening adopted by Central in conjunction with its block purchase of places. While the appointment of an individual to handle administration freed up the project manager from routine tasks, this in no way obviated the need for constant promotion.

The model of short-term care which has been adopted at Cairdeas House is of the planned break. In theory it avoids the crisis admission, although in practice it was possible to admit one individual at 24-hours notice when his wife and carer had to enter hospital. Guests during the survey period tended to be individuals with mental health problems themselves rather than their carers, although a week was used by older carers from Central. Moreover there have been few situations of carers themselves applying for the place for their relative or friend. If carers are to be encouraged to use the resource for their own needs there may have to be some careful targeting.

The testimony of the guests to date, however, as reported above and below, bears witness to both the support and 'fun' functions of Cairdeas House:

> 'I loved it from the bottom of my heart and will praise it to all I speak to.'

> 'I have been housebound for 11 months, was in depression. I came wanting to die, I left wanting to live. I never expected to be treated as a human being again and feel like one.'

> 'The house gives people suffering from illness and isolation a fantastic chance to get a nice break in a comfortable environment and treated with respect, which should give the individual a much needed boost to their confidence. Every city in the country should have one.'

Lest complacency strike, however, it should be remembered that, in the absence of similar models, for many of the guests expectations may have been relatively low. The challenges of ensuing months will be both to maintain the quality and energy of the provision, and to ensure it is taken on by a wider range of purchasers in order to clear the threat of closure:

> 'A place of unwinding beauty, that's Cairdeas House to me.'

References

Leff, J., Kuipers, L., Berkowitz, R., Eberlein-Vries, R. and Sturgeon, D. (1982) 'A controlled trial of social intervention in the families of schizophrenic patients.' *British Journal of Psychiatry 141*, 121–134.

Lindsay, M., Kohls, M. and Collins, J. (1993) *The Patchwork Quilt: A Study of Respite Care Services in Scotland*. Edinburgh: Social Work Services Inspectorate for Scotland.

Penumbra Discussion Paper on Respite Care (1989). Edinburgh: Penumbra. August.

Perring, C., Twigg, J. and Atkin, K. (1990) *Families Caring for People Diagnosed as Mentally Ill: The Literature Re-examined*. London: HMSO.

Scottish Office (1992) *National Assistance (Assessment of Resources) Regulations 1992: Regulations and Guidance*. Circular SW13/1992. Edinburgh: Social Work Services Group.

Twigg, J. and Atkin, K. (1994) *Carers Perceived: Policy and Practice in Informal Care*. Buckingham: Open University Press.

Chapter 10

Innovation in Supporting Adults with Learning Disabilities

Margaret Flynn, Lesley Cotterill, Lesley Hayes and Tricia Sloper

Introduction

'My daughter has suffered weight loss in different respite places...she always came back with a weight loss...when you group people together, staff aren't one-to-one. She had to be alert to what was going to happen. She once had to share a room with a girl she was afraid of and I don't think she slept at all. She came back with a black eye and her nose bled every morning for a week... During her stay they kept saying everything was all right. When we saw her we were shocked and they just said she'd been fretting. The long-stay hospital was a disaster as well. I couldn't bear to visit and my husband was distressed that every time he went she was hiding behind a sofa. She was only a child and she looked drugged. We thought if we can manage without resorting to drugs surely they can and they assured us they hadn't. It took three months to get her to smile and she didn't want to be touched. It gave her a terror of hospitals, doctors and nurses and she's not got over it. In contrast, the respite service she receives now, targeting adults with challenging behaviour, brings lots of joy. It's the first service she's had that thinks of her...the support worker knows my daughter's moods...she's her age...she tries lots of different things...she's got the enthusiasm. When my daughter's going out, she sits and waits by the window. She's never had that before. They've opened a new world to her and I see her differently...her understanding has deepened, she's more grown up and she reacts quicker. They try things with her that I wouldn't do and they work. I feel very vulnerable if I take her out somewhere and she causes a scene. She used to lie down and thank God that's gone... Now she gets all excited and it's obvious she looks forward to it. They understand that she's a one person person...'

The experiences of this woman and her daughter, and those of many other families, led to a bid for research funding from the Joseph Rowntree Foundation to learn more about different kinds of respite services in England. We assumed that the most typical type of respite is building based. As the quotation suggests, this has problems.

A context

In 1994, the National Development Team[1] was associated with the efforts of several agencies in reviewing and redeveloping their respite units for adults with learning disabilities. Broadly these services: accommodate no more than 30 women and men in a single year; have vacancies only if a respite user dies, is relocated in 'long stay' accommodation or leaves the locality; do not view the demarcation of children and adults as rigid; tend to overlook the galaxy of differences between people; view lost clothes as a fact of life; and have operating costs in excess of £200,000 at 1994 prices. The parents of the children, women and men using these units regard themselves as the primary beneficiaries of respite. The dominant expectation of respite – that it occurs in units largely established for this purpose – leads many to oppose vigorously any alternative candidates to respite as they know it. The death of a man in one unit, associated with such persistent operating failures as inadequate procedures for administering medication, accommodating people with violent behaviours alongside people with limited mobility, minimal staffing and supervision arrangements, did not unsettle the overriding certainty of the parent group that the unit only needed to employ better staff.

These parents are not wilfully wrong. Their vigorous efforts to champion respite as they know it have a history. This includes: respite being the only service offered to their daughters and sons; a prevailing 'use it or lose it' belief; the temporal regularity of familiar respite being

---

1   The National Development Team provides consultancy to voluntary organisations, health authorities and NHS Trusts, social services, education departments and training agencies in the UK. It offers advice about services for children, young people and adults with learning disabilities.

itself a relief; and wariness of 'reviews' which are euphemisms for discontinuing services.

What has all this got to do with 'innovative' respite services (Schwartz 1992)? It draws attention to the gauntlet which has to be run by emerging respite services which compel all of us to reconsider the ways support to people with learning disabilities is viewed. We know that the identification of innovative respite services is an inexact process. Not only is the adjective 'innovative' obstinately beyond the reach of precise definition in relation to service provision, but also, as previous chapters have shown, there is a lack of clarity about the term 'respite' and the roles of 'respite services'.

Starting from innovation

In the bid for research funding, we described one innovative service, Natural Breaks in Liverpool, which operates on the margins of unit-based respite provision and (in 1994) offered to 22 adults:

- person-to-person support;
- a focus on the mutual leisure interests of the service user and support worker;
- a commitment to being in ordinary places such as leisure centres, colleges and restaurants and staying in hotels and guest houses;
- an emphasis on positive links with people's families and friends;
- flexibility regarding individual and family circumstances;
- an investment in serving adults with substantial support needs and people whom specialist services had indicated a reluctance to serve.

The interest of Natural Breaks in introducing adults with learning disabilities to leisure activities, to new opportunities within their communities and, just as importantly, to other people, signalled to us a major shift in thinking about ways in which people are offered breaks. Insofar as Natural Breaks seeks to provide the sorts of breaks which are familiar to non-disabled people, it enlarged our understanding of what innovative respite services can be like. Accordingly, we sought to produce an inventory of respite services for adults with learning disabilities in England and to produce case-study narratives of innovative respite services.

A further influence was a study of innovation in a local authority by Bernard (1990). She highlighted those factors which are strongly associated with the adoption of innovation. These include: task and person-centred cultures; the availability of resources and, conversely, the drive for economy; the mechanisms for spreading innovation; information networks; innovations compatible with individual values; and direct experiences of innovation.

What we did

At the beginning of the study, we wrote to research and practitioner journals outlining our aim of building up a picture of respite services, including innovative services, for adults with learning disabilities in England (Hayes *et al.* 1995). We deliberately did not define 'innovative services'. Our requests for information from journal readers and from Social Services Departments (SSDs) completing survey questionnaires placed stress on them nominating innovative services.

Of the 76 SSDs who responded to the survey (out of 108), 32 reported knowledge of at least one service they considered innovative. From this and other sources, nine services were selected for particular scrutiny. It will be seen from the next section that our judgements were not always accurate.

The services focused largely on evenings and weekends every week and some offered daytime support to people for whom there were no alternatives. Natural Breaks and the family support team also had a holiday component. Although the services have a strong leisure/activity focus (see Figure 10.1) they are characterised by diversity (see also Chapter 4 of this volume).

Several SSDs cited their Adult Placement Schemes as innovative because of the individualised nature of this provision. While we recognised that the person-centred approaches of these schemes rendered them eligible for inclusion in the study, only one was selected. Further, we did not seek an average or typical Adult Placement Scheme, but rather one which might teach us something about the design of services around individuals.

- An activity/sports service for 48 people who do not have extensive support needs. People usually pursue activities in small groups with the support of a volunteer.

- Natural Breaks which match 22 people on the basis of shared interests with support workers. People are supported by one or more workers depending on their support needs.

- A domiciliary respite service for 29 people which offers both small-group support and one-to-one support.

- A sessional worker service which began as an adjunct to an Adult Placement Scheme which in turn resulted from a resettlement programme. This supports 26 people on a one-to-one basis.

- A befriending scheme supporting 66 people. The service seeks to establish friendships and specifically targets people from black and ethnic minority communities.

- A family-support team of qualified nurses working with 18 adults with challenging behaviours, extensive support needs and/or mental health problems. Each adult is matched with two nurse/support workers.

- A home-based support service for 17 adults.

- An Adult Placement Scheme for 25 people.

Figure 10.1 An outline of eight services

Two lessons

Two significant lessons emerged. First, definitions of respite services and innovative respite in particular, may not accord with the ideas of people with learning disabilities. In order to be credible to people with learning disabilities, we took the view that we had to be proactive in learning from them and from their experiences. The User Committee of a large day centre in Liverpool assisted in this process over a period of nine months (Flynn with Liverpool Self Advocates 1994). From visits to respite services, individual and group discussions, a series of service principles resulted. They are expressed in terms of what respite services should be like, i.e. they should:

1. enable people to have control

2. offer good experiences and personal advantages

3. sustain feelings of personal worth and esteem

4. be ordinary and separate from accommodation offered to people on a long-term basis

5. promote individual supports as a result of individual planning

6. sustain people's significant relationships and make links with their lives – particularly their diverse roles in their families

7. be local – even in emergencies

8. be responsive to the ideas and concerns of service users; and

9. part company with the dispiriting features associated with unit-based respite.

In turn, the study was strongly influenced by the contribution of Liverpool self advocates (see Chapter 2).

Second, there are problems with an identification process which relies heavily on self-reporting and reputation; for example innovation to one Unit General Manager was people with learning disabilities 'holidaying' in a designated, long-stay hospital ward. Thus we recast one of the nine services ultimately selected for the study as 'a once innovative service'.

This residential behavioural unit, which will be called 'The Pines', was established in 1985 by a District Health Authority to:

- address the needs of adults with learning disabilities

- prevent them entering long-term institutions

- build up compatible groups of people for long-term care.

Aspirations to be a service 'on demand' were crushed by the fact that all families were booking only weekends and holiday periods. Accordingly The Pines became more directive and required families to use the unit during weekdays and the less popular times. A formerly matched number of qualified and unqualified staff has altered, and in 1994 there were more unqualified staff than qualified (7:3). Since 1985 the number of service users has steadily increased to 23. Significantly, the number of staff and the budget allocated for the day-to-day running of the unit has not increased. Outreach work with people's families has not developed as originally planned, as the project leader explained:

> 'We do home visits but they [carers] don't like us to tell them what to do in their own homes... We said we'd go and look after people

in their own home, but we haven't got the staff...to go and baby-sit. We've only got two staff on at most.'

Although many parents value the break afforded by the unit, several are aware that now it struggles to offer an effective service which is valued by service users:

> 'We don't tell him he's going away 'cause when they get here he tells them to F off. Once he's there he's fine... He runs when he sees them. "No, no, no, home" he says. I was never happy about it.'

> 'As far as I'm concerned there's nothing else...I've got to feel happy about it. It's the only service. I have no other service to compare.'

Advantages have been realised by some adults with learning disabilities, including introductions to new activities and people. These are overshadowed, however, by the stresses and strains which now prevail: the diminishing availability of emergency respite; the unresolved irritations of lost clothing; the inability of people with learning disabilities and their parents to influence practice in the unit; the inactivity of residents; delays in repair work and refurbishment of 'The Pines' (as the Project Leader observed: 'I think I'm wasted here. Most of the time I'm painting walls'). Other problems include negligible staff turnover; the introduction of first, a sociable group, second, a quiet group and third, an aggressive group (which is extremely difficult for staff to work with); inadequate staffing overall; isolation from interdisciplinary support; fear of some service users by both staff and other service users; and estrangement from credible training and support.

Thus within a decade, a 'model' service had declined to disadvantage both people with learning disabilities and their parents. It had become inflexible, professionally determined and very narrow in terms of what it provided for people. Further, it bore no resemblance to the kinds of services sought by people with learning disabilities.

Some shared themes

In contrast to The Pines, the eight other services are characterised by diversity. They are new schemes insofar as two began providing services in the late 1980s and six since 1990. Their emergence had a lot to do with:

- local consultation, fact finding and networking
- awarding priority to the ideas and preferences of adults with learning disabilities and their carers
- an aspiration to offer something better than segregated leisure opportunities
- an aspiration to do more than unquestioningly reproduce existing respite services and/or a reluctance to tolerate the poor coverage of respite services.

Any development process has multiple causes. Three stand out as profoundly important, albeit to different degrees in respect of these services.

First, clearly transmitted aims and service philosophy borne of the ideas, preferences and experiences of people with learning disabilities and their families.

It was striking that the eight services demonstrated a readiness to learn from the experiences of people with learning disabilities. One parent said of the family-support team: 'It offers a completely different service geared to the clients and their needs, unlike a residential unit where individual attention is difficult and is more to give the carer some respite.'

Most services deliberately focus their work on evenings and weekends as the nurse team leader explained: 'We focused contact on evenings and weekends. That was because from Friday evening to Monday morning some people just didn't go out so were very isolated.'

For the users of the befriending scheme, links are made on the basis of shared cultural backgrounds. A worker explained:

> 'It's not like fostering because at the end of the day, we have friends from different cultural groups...but what is important is that people's individual cultural needs are being respected... their diet needs, their linguistic needs, their religious needs. That's important for everybody... we all have individual needs that make us individual.'

The co-ordinator of the activity/sports service stated: 'We saw the need for people to go out and do things.'

At the outset, parents had been keen to assist in the activities promoted by this service. Their offer was declined: 'We said no. We not only don't want you but you're not coming. Or, you can come once or for the first five minutes, but it's about you getting a break... it's very hard for them.'

It is striking that only the befriending scheme is unequivocal about the service being primarily for the service users. The other services more readily acknowledge that parents and carers, as service providers as well, also benefit.

The founders and co-ordinators of the eight services are qualified professionals. It is noteworthy that most retain involvement in service provision even though the administrative demands of their work have increased.

Second, an emphasis on building new relationships for people with learning disabilities which extend beyond their immediate families.

The co-ordinator of the befriending service observed:

> 'My work, when I first started, was very much talking to people with learning disabilities about what they wanted... People with learning disabilities were saying what they lacked was a one to one friendship... We take friendship for granted and what having a friend gives you. It gives you a value and self esteem to know that someone wants to spend time with you and to be special to you and that they're not there because they're paid to be there. They're there because they want to be there.'

A parent and a carer endorsed this:

> 'He's got everything material that he needs... but he hasn't got the young company. The service gives him the chance to go out and have fun with a lot of different people.'

> 'It has shown her that she can have a social life independent of myself.'

A woman service user said: 'I am better with just the one person.'

Third, a recognition that sharing leisure activities can realise additional advantages and opportunities for adults with learning disabilities and in turn, their parents and carers.

> 'Natural Breaks is a service that, it might sound crazy, brings families together... it's her own thing... with her using that service, she was coming back to me with things I didn't know and it was making our relationship stronger because we could talk about other things.'

'Mary used to walk with her head down. Now she isn't. Now she's standing up again and I think it's because she's got more confidence.'

'This service has enabled him to return to an ATC after an absence of approximately four years and to mix with people other than parents.'

'I asked if they'd help shopping for clothes. I used to bring clothes home for her to look at and try on. They don't. She shops with them and they've made her more modern looking. She doesn't fight with them like she did with me... They try different things to see how she reacts. They're opening up new things that we haven't – the young scene... they've got the enthusiasm... When we got together, every single parent said the Family Support Team had helped.'

'The thing that makes it special for me is that he can go out... socialise with people of his own age and he can participate in something different... His life isn't so humdrum, so boring, so predictable. There is something for him to look forward to.'

'It's given my daughter a new lease of life.'

'My son didn't leave the house for years and years. I couldn't even go to the toilet by myself. His favourite position was sitting next to me with his head on my shoulder. If it hadn't been for Natural Breaks we'd still be there. They got him out of the house and what's more, he enjoyed going out. I guarantee he'd never have gone to the hostel for respite. It changed my life.'

These views of parents are endorsed by support personnel. Their relationships and understanding of people's wishes and contact with people's parents and carers have enabled them to be imaginative in their work: 'There's a woman we support and she likes cleaning tables. We're exploring the possibility of her working in a cafe for half a day a week. We'll support her initially.'

A man who had never been able to visit his mother's grave has made this one focus of contact with his befriender. Extending networks to those of support workers is another element of some services. The befriending scheme has matched two Asian men, who had been isolated from their culture in residential units, with an Asian befriender.

This link has enabled them to discover a great deal about their culture and history, about family life and about friendships.

A critical stance

No services are free of difficulties and none of the services we visited is exemplary in every way. Thus, focusing attention on nine 'innovative' services did not remove the need to adopt a critical stance. In this section we outline three particular pitfalls which merit attention if services are to be credible in the long term to people with learning disabilities and their families.

First, it is evident from the 'two lessons' above that the diminishing capability of a once 'model' unit suggests that innovative services are in jeopardy if they are viewed as frozen configurations. Reputations are time-limited. That managers continue to flag-wave this unit as 'innovative' speaks of their isolation from the concerns of their employees and most particularly, from the lives of people with learning disabilities.

Second, with only one exception, the services outlined on p.159 have not prioritised the introduction of multi-level safeguards. The subject of abuse did not feature in most of the training programmes for support personnel; the manager of one service had not considered the possibility of abuse; and the co-ordinator of another stated that robust recruitment practices rendered it extremely unlikely. The assumptions informing these positions should concern us, not least because the safety of people with learning disabilities was a recurring theme in interviews with parents and carers. Further, it had particularly influenced the approach of the activity/sports service. This was being developed as evidence of sexual abuse was emerging in a local special school. Accordingly, parents had been anxious to ensure that their daughters and sons were not receiving one-to-one support. They took the view that there is safety in numbers or more specifically, in small groups.

As one parent said of her role:

'I'm her safeguard. I didn't want her to be involved with men – looking after her when there's no-one else there. I said to the co-ordinator I want her to be matched with women about her age... She's got no speech and she's got very challenging behaviours... I know she won't put up with things she doesn't want but she won't be able to let on what had happened to her... so I'm her safeguard and they know what I want for her.'

Third, most of the services we visited are aware of their impermanence. A number had been established through short-term funding, sometimes topped up with *ad hoc* grants. Levels of funding were not always adequate and this sometimes resulted in compromises being made. The concern that new and less-established services bear an undue share of financial cutbacks creates uncertainties. Thus some regard themselves as constrained in their potential because their financial bases are so tenuous.

Some conclusions

We began this chapter with a quotation which sharply exemplifies the contrast between respite in such congregate settings as a hospital or hostel for people with learning disabilities and a person-centred service. The latter is infrequently associated with respite services, as these are provided in units designated for this purpose or in hostels which combine long-stay accommodation with 'respite beds' i.e. the most typical form of respite available in England.

Efforts to learn more about innovation in respite services led us initially to nine very different services. One of these was subsequently dropped from the frame and recast as 'a once innovative service'. Of the remaining eight, some are more path-breaking than others. Their ways of working articulate their person-centred philosophies. They have the flexibility to provide a wide range of opportunities to people. This has made it possible for some people to establish relationships and loyalties independently of their parents and carers. Some relationships are credited with changing people's lives.

Significantly, most of the services do not define themselves narrowly. Rather than offering 'respite beds' on an emergency or pre-planned basis, these services get to know people and their families well. They learn from them and build on these relationships to advocate with them. Of course there are cautionary concerns, not least surrounding people's safety and longer term planning, particularly when funding is fragile, time-limited and fragmented. It is striking, however, that in their emphasis on building relationships, these services are thoroughly compatible with the known aspirations of adults with learning disabilities (Flynn and Liverpool Self Advocates 1994).

References

Bernard, J. (1990) *Innovation in a Local Authority Social Services Department: Content, Context and Process.* MA in Social Policy and Social Research, Polytechnic of East London.

Flynn, M.C. with Liverpool Self Advocates (1994) *Taking a Break – Liverpool's Respite Services for Adult Citizens with Learning Disabilities.* Manchester, National Development Team.

Hayes, L., Flynn, M., Cotterill, L. and Sloper, T. (1995) *Respite Services for Adult Citizens with Learning Disabilities.* Report submitted to the Joseph Rowntree Foundation.

Schwartz, D.B. (1992) *Crossing the River – Creating a Conceptual Revolution in Community and Disability.* Brookline Books.

The Contributors

Kirsten Stalker Kirsten Stalker has carried out extensive research into short-term care in different parts of the UK. From 1988 to 1991, she was based at the Norah Fry Research Centre at Bristol University, evaluating a range of short-term care facilities for disabled children. She has published and lectured widely in this field. Dr Stalker is now a Senior Research Fellow at the Social Work Research Centre, University of Stirling, where she leads a programme of research on Community Care, focusing on disability.

Margaret Flynn Margaret Flynn PhD is an Assistant Director of the National Development Team, an agency which provides advice and consultancy to those who plan, commission and provide services to people with learning disabilities in the UK. She holds a Fellowship with the Royal College of General Practitioners.

Angela Darnell, Ian Davies, Marilyn Pegram, Peter Skilbeck and Jean Smith Angela Darnell, Ian Davies, Marilyn Pegram, Peter Skilbeck and Jean Smith are members of the Holt Hall Self-Advocacy group.

Philippa Russell Philippa Russell is Director of the Council for Disabled Children at the National Children's Bureau and an Associate Director of the National Development Team for People with Learning Disabilities. She is Chair of the Mental Health Foundation's Committee on children with learning disabilities and severely challenging behaviour and a member of the Prince of Wales's Advisory Group on Disability. In 1990 she was awarded the Rose Fitzgerald Kennedy Centenary International Award for women who have contributed to the field of a learning disability. She has worked on the development of guidance on children with disabilities and special educational needs relating to both the Children Act 1989 and the Code of Practice and Education Act 1993. Last, but by no means least, she is the parent of a young man with a learning disability and is associated with a wide range of voluntary and parent organisations throughout and beyond the UK.

Ann Netten Ann Netten is a Research Fellow at the Personal Social Services Research Unit, University of Kent at Canterbury. She worked in local authority social services research before joining the Unit in 1987. Much of her work has focused on costing, covering such diverse areas as health and social services, informal health care and the criminal justice system. Her other interests include care of older people, particularly environmental aspects of residential care and developing theoretical approaches to the evaluation of community care.

Meg Lindsay Meg Lindsay is a qualified Social Worker, with an honours degree in psychology. After working in adoption and fostering, in the 1980s she moved to Barnardo's, to establish a pioneering project for teenagers with profound learning disabilities. She has designed and managed both family-based and residential respite care services. In 1993, she completed a study for the Scottish Office into respite care services throughout Scotland, and is currently undertaking research into the service user's view of different forms of respite care. Previously Assistant Director of Social Work for NCH Action for Children in Scotland, she is now Director of the Centre for Residential Child Care and a Social Work Advisor for the Scottish Hospital Advisory Service.

Carol Robinson Carol Robinson is a Senior Research Fellow and Project Director at the Norah Fry Research Centre, University of Bristol. She was previously a social worker for Essex County Council, and carried out a PhD in the School of Education at Bristol University before joining its Department of Mental Health in 1983. Over the last ten years, she has conducted a number of research projects on short-term care for disabled children and has published many articles, pamphlets and a book on the subject.

Marie Bradley Marie Bradley is a Practitioner-researcher in child care. She has worked as a Social Worker with children and families, as an IT Officer with adolescents – which included numerous expeditions to the Welsh mountains – as a Counsellor in a large comprehensive school, and as a Lecturer in child development and child welfare. She currently works as a Research Associate with Professor Jane Aldgate and continues to work and to train in direct psychodynamic work with children.

Jane Aldgate Jane Aldgate is Professor of Social Work Studies at Leicester University. She has written extensively about children in foster care and residential care, and is especially interested in the implementation of partnership arrangements under the Children Act 1989. She is currently researching the definition of 'need' by local authorities, and the provision of services for the support of children and families in need.

Carole Archibald Carole Archibald has been involved in dementia care for approximately ten years. For four of these years she worked as a specialist Health Visitor at the Royal Edinburgh Hospital. This work comprised arranging daycare, respite and long- term

care. It involved a great deal of counselling and the setting up
of support groups for carers. Her work at the Dementia
Services Development Centre (DSDC) at Stirling University is
directed more towards professional carers. Ms Archibald's
main focus is development, although her work spills over into
all areas of the Centre's activity – research, training and
information provision. Her publications include *Sexuality and
Dementia and Activities 1 and 2*, books targeted very much
towards 'hands on' practitioners.

Alison Petch   Alison Petch has pursued a research career embracing a range of
social welfare issues. From 1986 to 1993 she was at the Social
Work Research Centre at Stirling University, developing a
particular interest in mental health research and establishing
the community care theme within the Centre. She was
appointed in 1993 to the newly established Nuffield Chair in
Community Care Studies at Glasgow University. The Nuffield
Centre aims to be a centre of excellence for the evaluation,
promotion and dissemination of community care practice.

Lesley Cotterill   Lesley Cotterill was awarded her PhD from the University of
Manchester in 1993 and has since published the thesis in a book
entitled *The Social Integration of People with Schizophrenia*
(Avebury, Aldershot, 1994). She has worked as a Research
Associate at the Hester Adrian Research Centre, University of
Manchester on a Joseph Rowntree funded project about respite
services for adults with learning disabilities and as a Research
Fellow in the Health Research and Development Unit,
Manchester Metropolitan University. In September 1994, she
took up an appointment as a Lecturer in the Department of
Sociology, Social Policy and Social Work Studies, University of
Liverpool and is now working as a Research Fellow in the
Health and Community Care Research Unit, University of
Liverpool.

Lesley Hayes   Lesley Hayes was Research Associate at the Hester Adrian
Research Centre until 1995 when she was appointed Research
Fellow in the Department of Pharmacy, Policy and Practice at
the University of Keele. She is involved in work on asthma,
gastroenterology and breast cancer.

Tricia Sloper   Tricia Sloper is Lecturer in Behavioural Science in the
Department of Public Health and Epidemiology, University of
Manchester, and Deputy Director of the Cancer Research
Campaign Education and Child Studies Research Group. She
has worked for many years at the Hester Adrian Research
Centre, in research on the needs of families of children with
disabilities, particularly families of children with Down's
Syndrome. More recently, she has also been concerned with
research on the needs of children in families affected by cancer.